Medieval Knowledge of the Compass

"Mariners at sea, when through cloudy weather in the day which hides the sun, or through the darkness of the night, they lose the knowledge of the quarter of the world to where they are sailing, though a needle with a magnet, which will turn round till, on its motion ceasing, its point will be directed towards the north."

Alexander of Neckham 1187-1202

"You will be able to direct your steps to cities and islands and to any place whatever in the world."

Pierre de Maricourt
Epistola de Magnete 1269

Both quotes taken from -

The Secret Dossier of a
Knight Templar of the Sangreal

by *Gretchen Cornwall*

Pages 177 & 178

The Templar Quest
to North America
a
Photo Journal

by
Gretchen Cornwall

https://gretchencornwall.com/

Grapevine Press Ltd.
February 25, 2020
Revised Edition -
due to new cover

The Templar Quest
to North America
a
Photo Journal

New Cover Edition

Grapevine Press Ltd.
Originally Published October 13th 2019

Published as a Color Hardback
ISBN: 978-1-912971-13-8
&
Published as a Color Paperback
ISBN: 978-1-912971-14-5

Kindle Available on Amazon
ISBN: 978-1-912971-08-4

Book Cover by Grapevine Press Ltd

Cover Photo of Knight Templar Courtesy of
George Emanuel Runer (Lord Knight)

Cheif Etow Oh Koam, Mahican, by Jan Verelst 1710

The moral right of Gretchen Cornwall to be identified as the author of this work has been asserted in accordance with the Copyright, Designs and Patents Act, 1988.

All rights reserved.
No part of this publication may be reproduced or transmitted in any form or by any means, electronic or mechanical, including photocopying, recording, or any information storage and retrieval system, without permission in writing from the publisher,
Grapevine Press Ltd.

https://gretchencornwall.com/

Contents

	Photo Credits	X
	Acknowledgements	XII
	Introduction	XV
	Preface	XVIII
1	Knights Templar & Oak Island	1
2	Vikings & Oak Island	7
3	Templar Cross Pattée	16
4	The Weight of Discovery	27
5	A Fading Way of Life	32
6	Into the Forest	40
7	The Knight Stone	44
8	The Cave	57
9	Follow the River	62
10	Oak Island Carvings	66
11	Brave Allies	74

Contents

12	A Day at the Museum	80
13	Research	86
14	Mound Builders	92
15	Roche-A-Cri Park	94
16	We The People	106
17	The Lost Temple in the Woods	109
18	Wisconsin's Templar Castle	111
19	The Triangle of the Knight Stone	117
20	The Knight Stone Reveals Itself	125
21	The Templar Tomb	134
22	The Wisconsin Templar Preceptory	161
23	Homeward Bound	166
24	A Special Thank You	172
	Selected Bibliography	174

Partial Photo Credits

Note: All photos were taken either by myself, Gretchen Cornwall or Mr. Wayne Murphy. Paintings older than 75 years have not been credited due to space and are freely available to view online along with other commonly used icons and graphics. Otherwise, credit is given in the body of the text or here on the next two pages. If an omission has occurred please contact Gretchen Cornwall so that a credit may be given online:

https://gretchencornwall.com/

*All photos taken of George Emanuel Runer - Lord Knight by Evelyn Rosario Runer M.D.

1   George Emanuel Runer - Lord Knight

5   Templar Flag Shutterstock Illustration ID: 1179726001

11 Map by Max Naylor

13 Kensington Runestone by George T. Flom 1910

14 Viking Ship Shutterstock Illustration ID: 515156236

15 Viking Woman Shutterstock Illustration ID: 478449772

18 George Emanuel Runer - Lord Knight

31 Native American Brave Shutterstock Illustration 64503115

49 George Emanuel Runer - Lord Knight

Partial Photo Credits

56   George Emanuel Runer - Lord Knight & Knight Stone

67   Brave & Canoe Shutterstock Illustration ID: 96268730

71   Overton Stone on Oak Island, Courtesy of Terry J. Deveau

75   Herm Stone, Courtesy of Alessandra Nadudvari

75   3-D Herm Stone, Courtesy of Doug Crowell

93   George Emanuel Runer - Lord Knight

119 King Etow Oh Koam, Mahican, by Jan Verelst 1710

125 Tetragrammaton at Versailles by P. Vasilliadis

George Emanuel Runer - Lord Knight:
pages: 118, 125, 128, 158, 160, 163, 172, 173
Photography by Evelyn Rosario Runer M.D.

Acknowledgements

I want to thank Wayne Murphy for his courage in taking a photo and sending it across the Atlantic to myself. I appreciated Mary Murphy's hospitality and lovely home while I stayed with her active household for twelve days in June & July of 2019.

Larry P. Madden for his generosity of time and knowledge of the Great People he represents on the Mohican Nation Stockbridge-Munsee Reservation of Wisconsin.

I owe much to my family, friends and inspirational acquaintances I've met along the way - without their valiant encouragement my work would lack a colorful light.

John Cornwall thank you for your continuing friendship, music and coffee.

Thank you Mother Divine, Marcia Winter, for instilling within the love of books at a young age. I'll always treasure our trips to the library together and seeing you read in your chair late into the night searching for the answers to mysteries.

For my Father Volunteer Fireman-

Assistant Chief, Lee Schroeder, who cared enough to save lives as a volunteer. I admire your faith and ethos of service to others. Carole Schroeder, I appreciate your grace, patience and love.

To my siblings who are also my best friends – Shirley, Raymond, Judith, Ruth and Tracy. They are remarkable people who fight the good fight to make their dreams come true. They serve their communities and are mirrors of life which I respect and hold dear.

With gratitude to my friend Serena Lowman for her generosity in research, as a sounding board and friend. John Nugent for his friendship and sound commentary.

Marie Clewley, thank you for your wisdom and inspiring and beautiful messages.

Doug Crowell, Paul Troutman, Judi Rudebusch and the intrepid Oak Island team, may the sun always shine on your path. Rick & Marty Lagina, thank you for your courtesy and professionalism for all those captivated with your island adventures.

Without the friendship of Grail composer Adrian Wagner and Helen Wagner, I would not be living in England. Author Laurence Gardner who lit the fuse to my journey.

Thank you to all those authors who have dug deeper than the veneer of shallow authority and had the courage to plunge down the rabbit hole with Alice. You've carried us all with you...

Thank you Lord Knight, George Emanuel Runer for bringing the Templars alive in your photos! I appreciate your Eagle Eye & editing talents. I may not have taken on board all suggestions, but you are a detail master of grammar! Many thanks to Evelyn Rosario Runer M.D. for wonderful photos of a great knight!

To those who have stood on the shoulders of giants in centuries past so that we have a continued thread to follow through the maze of history and clues as to what it means to be truly human. You've pointed the way to our future-

To the Knights Templar Order who have never left the field.

Introduction

I've been in the fortunate position of studying the Knights Templar since the mid 1990's. I don't believe that interest in the ill fated knights will ever wane, it's actually growing.

They are front and center in the consciousness of millions today through documentaries, film, blogs, and books.

The gain in awareness is on equal footing with King Arthur's Camelot and as epic a romance and tragedy. Indeed there may be direct ties between the Templars and the Knights of the Round Table, but that investigation of fact and fantasy is for another day.

The Templar Quest
to North America - a Photo Journal

During the last few years I've been approached by earnest people who believe they have found physical evidence of the Templars in North America.

It sounds fantastical on the face of it, however, there is actual basis for the re-examination of the Pre-Columbian discovery story. I found one discovery in particular so compelling that I had to follow it up.

I am not the first author to assert that Templar voyages to the New World occurred. But it is my hope that this book serves the growing body of physical evidence for the case of the Knights Templar and their secret ongoing missions in North America during the medieval era.

Introduction

In the summer of 2018, I was sent photos that would lead me to the now Tribal lands of the Mohicans.

The initial photo was of a Templar Cross Pattée via Facebook Messenger. I nearly fell out of my chair. It was credible and the individual who sent them had such an integrous background as to be the stuff of movies! Wayne Murphy, retired police officer and Tribal Elder of the Mohicans, was not given to flights of fancy.

I had to visit the location myself and meet the man who found the carving to verify the discovery, but found so much more as to exceed my expectations at the site. I determined that I may have been standing on the grounds of a lost Templar settlement near Lake Michigan, deep in the woods on the Mohican Reservation.

The growing realization of what had been achieved in such a dangerous voyage and inland exploration by Templars could only mean that they had Native American allies.

The site was not just a random carving but the beginnings of what I believed could be an actual Templar relay fortress for the purpose of a westward push and a sustained return.

The dramatic history of the Templars rise and fall has become familiar. The infamous date of October 13th, 1307. A day that shocked Europe and gave us the folklore of bad luck down the centuries, known as Friday the 13th.

Did they survive? Where did they go? What were their hopes and dreams for the future? I believe the investigation held within the pages of this book answers many of these questions.

Gretchen Cornwall
October 13, 2019

Preface

A note from the author

I believe that the anomalies of history are worth investigating. Rather than sweeping them under a carpet to preserve the status quo, oddities should be regarded as mounting evidence for a historical course correction. Anomalies are an opportunity to deepen our understanding of who we are and our origins.

It is far too simplistic to walk past an object, architectural feature or an odd local legend as being circumstantial. Dig just below the surface and narrow dull threads turn into golden ropes of probabilities...

I have long been a proponent of Templar missions to North America. I was approached by Wayne Murphy, in July of 2018 with a photograph of a rock carving that had every earmark of being medieval Templar graffiti. I knew I had to jump in with both feet and find out all that was possible about his mysterious discovery -

Note: I chose to honor the two different spellings used for the Mohican tribe. They themselves use both spellings of either Mohican or Mahican. Since it is their own self-description, it is not a spelling error to use either Noun.

Two Knights Templar playing chess -

- As each day progressed the complexity of the site grew in importance...

Gretchen Cornwall

October 13, 2019

New Cover Edition: February 25, 2020

One

Knights Templar & Oak Island

In my first book, The Secret Dossier of a Knight Templar of the Sangreal, I strove to unearth the details of Templar survivors and the hidden roots of their past.

I highlighted the many ports where Knights were potentially able to flee for shelter, both in Europe and in North America.

In some cases, they stayed where they were and changed their name with the support of a local sympathetic monarch, happy to receive highly trained knights, their knowledge and wealth.

The most famous of these monarchs was Robert the Bruce of Scotland. Legends of mysterious white knights have followed the king through history. Riding into battle, saving his kingdom from the English at the Battle of Bannockburn in 1314 on the feast day of St. John the Baptist, the patron saint of the Templar order.

I have avidly followed The Curse of Oak Island, which first aired on the History Channel, January of 2014, due to my interest in the survival of the Knights Templar.

They were arrested en masse in 1307 and imprisoned for several further years. They lost their Grand Master and two of his senior officers in a horrific execution in 1314, ending the public face of the tough, skilful and most mysterious Order in Europe.

Opposite - George Emanuel Runer, Lord Knight

The Templar Quest
to North America - a Photo Journal

The courage of Jacques de Molay at his execution by fire had to leave an indelible mark on the minds of those who survived.

Knights Templar & Oak Island

This investigation is one avenue of inquiry as to what happened to the survivors.

I had the privilege of being in the War Room of the Curse of Oak Island, virtually, in Season Six, Episode Six 2018.

I am proud to have shared research with the Oak Island team behind the scenes and wish them all the best in their quest to discover what may have happened in centuries past. And of course, we all want them to find the big golden smoking gun!

The Templar Quest
to North America - a Photo Journal

The Last Grand Master of the Knight Templar Order
Jacques de Molay - Executed March 1314

I am thrilled by their weekly archaeological finds and view each as an incredible historical treasure, each unique as if they were peeling the centuries back year by year.

It was through The Curse of Oak Island that I became aware of the author, Zena Halpern, who has sadly passed after publishing her first book at the age of 85! A great achievement at any age, let alone the later years of one's life - a testament to her zeal, energy and love of history.

Knights Templar & Oak Island

I recommend her book 'The Templar Mission to Oak Island and Beyond'.

I concur with her that the Templars had been on Oak Island and that one of the possible draws to the area was that of Gold River, Nova Scotia, due north of Oak Island.

Templars could have discovered a source of gold from the river which may have been part of the secret of their wealth.

The Beauséant Battle Flag of the Templars
Shutterstock.com stock illustration ID: 1179726001

Two
Vikings & Oak Island

How in the world did Templars come to Oak Island? Their predecessors the Vikings showed them the way and passed down their knowledge. Detailed information on this subject will be shared in a later volume.

L'Anse aux Meadows in Newfoundland is the site of a Norse (AKA Viking) failed settlement dated to 1000 AD.

It has been surmised as being a vessel repair station. This implies that a larger population surrounded the repair station, justifying the need for a settlement with one purpose.

There may be proof of this in years to come as archaeologists continue to explore the surrounding lands around the repair station.

Newfoundland is not far at all from Oak Island for experienced sea-faring Vikings. It is situated north along the eastern coastline of Canada.

Opposite -
The Saking of Paris in 845 AD
by Viking Chieftain, Ragnar Lothbrok
19th century

The Templar Quest
to North America - a Photo Journal

In the year 1066, the last and greatest Viking, William the Conqueror took the English throne by force bringing to a close the Viking raids in Europe forever.

He was the Duke of Normandy a Prince of the Norse, or men of the north. His ancestor, Duke Rollo, was given the title by the desperate King of Paris who was tired of the Vikings raiding his kingdom.

So, the King of the Franks gave the savvy raiders land at the mouth of the river Seine to protect it from fellow Vikings. He gave Rollo a title and marriage into the royal family in 911 AD. The King of Paris had conquered the Vikings to mutual benefit.

The overlapping of these events must include the voyages of Leif Erikson the Norse explorer of 970 AD to 1020 AD famed for discovering the fabled Vinland. It is now accepted that Erikson found North America 500 years before Columbus, including the mouth of the St. Lawrence River.

One of the navigation aids used by Vikings was the sunstone. "The legendary 'sunstone' mentioned in ancient Viking writings was thought to be a myth; a magical talisman that aided the captain at times when the sun was behind the clouds." pg 350 The Secret Dossier of a Knight Templar of the Sangreal

If this seems far-fetched that the Vikings used Optical Calcite to find North America and even more preposterous that the Sinclair's did so; then what was a specimen doing in a captains navigation box, found on board a sunken Elizabethan warship?

Knowledge of North America was now in the royal courts of France and also England through Rollo and his descendant-

Two
Vikings & Oak Island

Optical Calcite Sample Thanks to Serena Lowman
Gretchen Cornwall Photo

The Templar Quest
to North America - a Photo Journal

Optical Calcite
Author Gretchen Cornwall

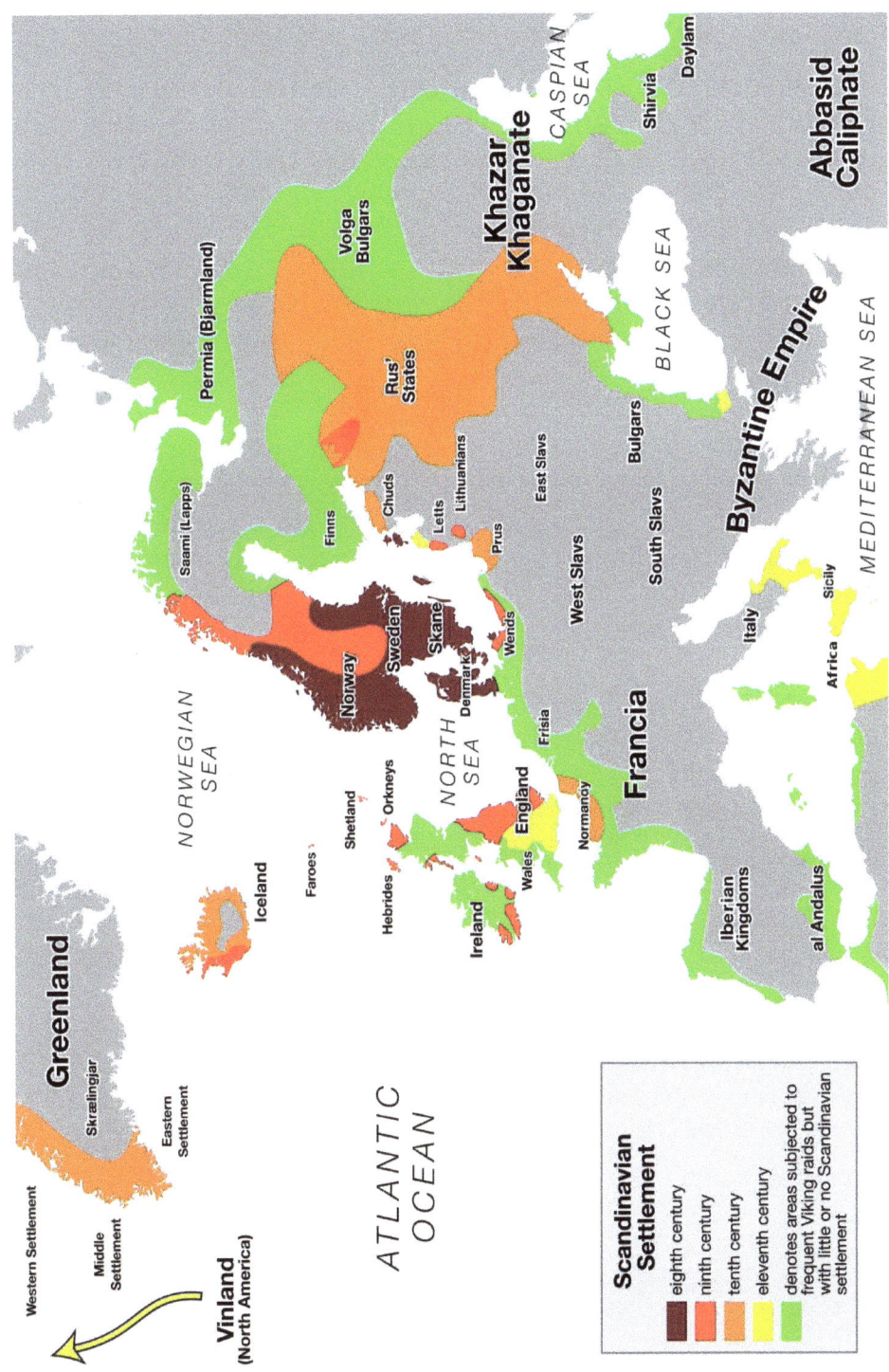

The Templar Quest
to North America - a Photo Journal

- King William, but still regarded as a secret. At varying times both English and French kingdoms were ruled by the same families with a shared flow of information as a result.

The Norse were everywhere in the known world as their sailing knowledge was beyond compare. They were never conquered by Rome and voluntarily became Christian to increase their trade, wealth and status, sometimes through marriage.

The cross over period of Norse Pagan art into Christian art is fascinating as is their written language, the Runes. Hints of this language are strewn about North America, a sure sign that 'Sven was here.' Their language was complex and represented not only the written word but entire philosophical concepts.

The strange language encoded in stone, on the eastern seaboard of North America, having been changed from the Runic into code form known only to those who were meant to understand and take action upon carvings.

Traces of this writing have been discovered on Oak Island as Vertical Ciphers/Codes and indeed further west into Minnesota where the Kensington Runestone was found and translated as possibly dating to 1362 AD.

Author Scott Wolter has done a great deal of work on the Kensington Runestone and also broke ground on the significant Hooked X, amongst other Templar related discoveries.

http://scottwolteranswers.blogspot.com/

https://www.amazon.co.uk/Kensington-Rune-Stone-Compelling-Evidence/dp/1975623878/ref=sr_1_fkmr0_2?keywords=kensington+runestone%2C+scott+wolter&qid=1566644152&s=gateway&sr=8-2-fkmr0

Two
Vikings & Oak Island

George T. Flom
Images of the two carved faces of the Kensington Runestone, from George Flom's short book
"The Kensington Rune-Stone" (Illinois State Historical Society, 1910)

The Templar Quest
to North America - a Photo Journal

History is taught in isolated chunks or units for ease of classroom understanding and time limitations. Episodes of cause and effect over centuries are disconnected from each other, in reality, a pattern emerges when viewing all elements as a row of dominoes.

The men of the north, having merged with French, Scottish and English Kingdoms passed their resources and knowledge down to the next generation out of the so-called Dark Ages to the hands of the capable, adventurous Knights Templar.

Three
Templar Cross Pattée

The Templar Cross Pattée is specific to the Order and though it is an equilateral cross which is a global symbol for the sun in many cultures; the Cross Pattée is the unique emblem of the Poor Fellow-Soldiers of Christ and of the Temple of Solomon.

It was adopted by the Teutonic Knights and kingdoms that had strong Templar influences, if not actual ruler-ship, such as Switzerland and Portugal.

Early sources show the cross as being of a simpler design used by Templars:

https://commons.wikimedia.org/wiki/File:Cross_of_the_Knights_Templar.svg

Three
Templar Cross Pattée

Later designs by the Templars varied with the arms splayed outward and larger on the outer edges and narrowing at the center.

I have seen variations in Templar churches in France & England with the below as graphical examples:

Three
Templar Cross Pattée

Templars were permitted to wear the white robes of their cousins, the Cistercians, and to adorn the mantle with a red cross above the heart.

The entire focus of my research and work changed when I received the Facebook Message from Wayne Murphy, asking what my thoughts were on his attached photo of what he thought might be a Templar Cross Pattée. And could I affirm or disregard it?

I struggled with the single photo I received. The granite stone was rosy, but speckled with black and other variants of color. It made the depth perception difficult and identification rather trying. Add to it the lichen - Clearly, I had a major task on my hands.

Opposite - George Emanuel Runer, Lord Knight

Three
Templar Cross Pattée

...But with that said there were clear indications of a severely eroded cross within the first image, but was it Templar?

I felt that the degree of erosion was appropriate for a carving of 700 years or more and that the raised bevelled edges were European techniques requiring great skill. Native Americans did not have tools capable of producing a carving of this nature.

The Templar Quest
to North America - a Photo Journal

What then followed were several phone calls and requests on my part for further images and information on the area.

I also needed to know more about the individual who discovered the carving. Conversely, Wayne Murphy needed to know he could trust me with his images, would I do justice with the project and verify what he had encountered?

In the months that followed, Wayne sent further photos of his location:

Three
Templar Cross Pattée

The image opposite is a circular carving of raised edges with an equilateral cross within.

Three
Templar Cross Pattée

Wisconsin experiences harsh winters with snow of five feet, and even higher snowdrifts with scorching summer heat.

The contraction of severe snow and opposite heat expansion, alone over centuries, would erode a carving that stood unprotected in the elements.

The difficulty in viewing the carving in the photos is consistent with its age and verifies it. The raised edges are not a cooperation of nature, but that of a skilled human hand.

It brought to my mind a Templar Cross Pattée highlighted in the documentary series - Buried: Knights Templar and the Holy Grail. Produced for the History Channel:
https://www.history.co.uk/shows/buried/articles/buried-episodes

In the final episode, 'Four, Land of Secrets', hosts, Mikey Kay, and Garth Baldwin, are confronted with an eroded Templar cross where none should exist in a church in Portugal.

It had been hidden behind plaster, covered over for centuries. The cross was only visible in certain lighting and not always viewable with the naked eye.

On the day of filming, they were very fortunate they could see the cross and commented during the interview that it was very subtle and hard to view -

I highly recommend watching the four episodes which back up my assertions that the Templars survived. Noted scholar, Dan Jones, provided academic context and information for the two hosts who used their military skills and archaeological background to comprehend the movements of the Templars after the arrests of 1307.

The Templar Quest
to North America - a Photo Journal

I was pleased to see a documentary that covered the brilliant and often overlooked St. Bernard de Clairvaux. He was the mind behind the Templars and the Kingdom of Portugal, or as stated in the documentary the Port of the Grail. To my knowledge, my book, The Secret Dossier of a Knight Templar of the Sangreal, spends more time investigating St. Bernard than any other author to date.

Apparition of the Virgin to St. Bernard de Clairvaux
Filippino Lippi, Florence

Four
The Weight of Discovery

Mr. Murphy sent a few photos during the winter of 2018 that showed the state of his extensive, party-worthy decking behind his home. One could entertain a wedding reception on the solid structure.

It had, however collapsed under the weight of an extreme winter snowfall, that had affected the entire Midwest and Eastern Seaboard.

I was beginning to be concerned about his potential cross discovery and what would remain of it between these harsh seasonal swings.

Mr. Murphy was also struggling with himself. Is it possible that he had indeed found evidence of Templar, Pre-Columbian contact, penetrating so far westward?

Would anyone believe him? Was he irresponsible or just ignorant? Would I think he was crazy and setting a trap for myself? After all, I did not know him or his family.

The weight of responsibility for such a find is greater than one would imagine, especially in the eye of one's family and friends.

To further complicate matters the carvings he discovered are on the Mohican Reservation of which he was a Tribal Elder. How would the tribe receive this news? Gladly or with trepidation? Would it be entirely ignored by his people? Would he be brushed off?

Verification from an experienced outside source was paramount if he were to be taken seriously.

The Templar Quest
to North America - a Photo Journal

We also had a duty of care to the location itself. France has had to create laws making it illegal to dig for treasure around the area of Rennes le Château.

The number of foolhardy and silly people showing up with shovels was ridiculous and ruining the landscape not to mention private property.

We've decided to keep the actual location a secret to protect it from being defaced, vandalized or disturbed.

The possibility of injury from being at the site is genuine if one could even find it.

Intensive exploration of the site would need to be completed by archaeologists and anthropologists in conjunction with tribal permissions.

The issue is rather sticky as the current Mohican tribe was moved onto the land in the early 19th century.

The Menominee would have been the original People that the Templars would have encountered in Wisconsin along with their guides from the Eastern Seaboard.

As an exciting and synchronistic circle, the Templars would have met the Mohicans in the valley of the Hudson River. And the other potential would have been the Mi'kmaq tribe.

Opposite - a Menominee Warrior
Amiskquew
by Charles Bird King (1785-1862)

The Templar Quest
to North America - a Photo Journal

I had many conversations with Mr. Murphy discussing the serious ramifications of the cross carvings while I was involved with other research.

I understood that the only way this was going to move forward was with my own two feet on the site. So I invested in a flight to meet him, his family, and his carvings in person.

It was essential to be respectful of the tribal lands, its people and history. Knowing this full well, it would have been irresponsible to voice Mr. Murphy's discovery without first evaluating the carving in case it was merely wishful thinking on his part.

I tried to balance out any excitement with practicality and a wait and see attitude. Failing to prove a significant historical find would be disappointing but could lead to great new friends on the other side of the adventure.

More data needed to be collected before raising the flag as this was a very serious claim, and it needed to be verified first.

I was not new to Native American history concerning early contact with either Vikings or Templars. The Mi'kmaq tribe may indeed have glimpses of this contact within their legends and religion.

The differentiation is so significant between the equal sun cross of the Native American Peoples and that of Knights Templar. There most certainly would be a crossover of culture and alliances, perhaps even marriages. I hoped to be able to cross the Atlantic and identify a Templar Knight Cross.

I chose to use the painting of Mohican Chief-King, Etow Oh Koam, on the cover of the book, as I found it impossible to find a photograph of a historically accurate Northeastern Woodland Tribal Leader. The majority of images available are of Western Peoples with fantastic headdresses. Regardless, this painting is fantastic. The King visited England with three other Chiefs. Painting by Jan Verelst 1710 AD.

Five
A Fading Way of Life

The flight from London Heathrow airport to Milwaukee Wisconsin was not straight forward due to a lack of direct flights.

Door to door, with a stopover in Chicago of four hours, was a 22-hour journey. Needless to say, I was a bit off-kilter when I arrived in Milwaukee.

Wayne Murphy picked me up in his ubiquitous pickup truck. Anyone living in the area who did not have a truck or SUV became stuck in the wild weather swings of the Wisconsin wilderness. It was a three-hour drive north to his family home.

I'm sure I must have looked somewhat glazed, but adrenaline helped me to adjust quickly to the time change. The thought of following in the footsteps of the Knights Templar in North America is heady indeed. I was ready to meet them!

During the ride north from the airport, and in the days that followed, I learned a great deal about Mr. Murphy, his family heritage, and his love of the Reservation that flowed in his veins.

The Templar Quest
to North America - a Photo Journal

He was born and raised in a forest. There are not too many people today that can make that claim. I was shown the family cabin, now in a state of sad disrepair, abandoned by the twists and turns of life.

He lived a life that most would describe as 'out of the past' and not to be repeated by most, except those brave souls who choose to live off-grid. His upbringing was not a choice. Hunting for this man and his family was a necessity in his youth, not a weekend privilege.

The cabin had no mod cons, of course. It reminded me of the time I visited the historic museum parkland that was in the forest of the Smokey Mountains of Tennessee where one could see restored cabins from the 19th century.

One of the reasons I decided to take the flight was Mr. Murphy's gravitas as a 'witness.' He was with the Milwaukee Police Department for 25 years, retiring as a Sergeant of 17 years. He'd served as a Federal Game Warden, spent two years in the Sheriff's Department and one year with Homeland Security Federal Protective Services.

He was honored with a 'Where As' from the City of Milwaukee Common Council for major arrests in homicide.

He sounded level, straight and knowledgeable on the phone. Not to mention that the photo he sent of the carving should not have existed.

He shared stories from his work as an officer that verified for myself the police dramas in film and television as art imitating life. He'd seen it all, and sometimes those

Five
A Fading Way of Life

memories were haunting. Protecting others came at the cost of his peace of mind. There are some things that one cannot unlearn or 'un-see'. They are etched on the mind.

Having found comfort in his faith, beautiful wife and family, proud of his home, Mr. Murphy looks forward in hope and armed with a great sense of humor.

There was nothing erratic or fantastical in his psyche. He was rooted by his pragmatic upbringing in the forest and the realities of working decades in the police force and investigating fraud.

In him, I found one of the best examples of service unto others. He also was a very talented musician, singer & songwriter, having performed as the lead singer for his band, supporting headliner acts in the broader area. I found Wayne to be a talented, intelligent, and a diverse individual with his feet on the ground who put family and community first.

When I arrived in late June, the weather was swinging from intolerably hot to torrential downpours, but it all seemed to flow to our advantage. I came prepared for all eventualities except snow of course for which I was grateful.

The Templar Quest
to North America - a Photo Journal

Five
A Fading Way of Life

The Murphy Family Cabin on the
Mohican Reservation
Wisconsin

Circumstances beyond the control of the Murphy Family has caused the cabin to be left unattended.

Five
A Fading Way of Life

On day one, he gave me a tour of the Reservation via the road network some of which were only logging roads. It was massive and I was soon lost -

I saw more deer, foxes, birds of every description, bear markings, bees, insects, little snakes... You name it! Owls were hooting in the night, cranes gracing the day... It would have been easy to stop and turn my attention to a wildlife documentary.

At times along the roadway, there had to have been 20 deer easily. He was very conscientious and with great care, looked for deer and fawns, knowing that it would be far too easy to hit one. Wayne was not a mean individual. I could see he respected the balance of nature.

I'd never seen so much wildlife everywhere I turned. I had grown up in the greater Seattle area, famed for its natural beauty and had not seen this abundance of wildlife in Washington State. It was a reminder that he and his family lived a long way from what most would call 'civilization.'

I did not see mountain lions or bears, but I was shown their travel signs. The Templars would have been met with like experiences and thought the new land to be full of promise, survivable if not sustaining.

We waited for the thunderstorms to pass and in a few days made our first trip into the woods.

The next page includes images from the surrounding area, old Victorian buildings no longer in use, testament to the passage of time and the history of the area.

The Templar Quest
to North America - a Photo Journal

Five
A Fading Way of Life

Six
Into the Forest

While I was armed with cameras and Deet, having soaked my clothing in Permethrin to keep the ticks and mosquitoes at bay, Wayne, who knows the woods, was prepared to meet bears, mountain lions and be able to lead through dangerous unmarked terrain.

My investigation was placed square in the middle of high mosquito season, which I was to learn, is a real drawback when looking for signs of a lost Templar exploration party. I have to admit the mosquitoes were everywhere and awful.

I was grateful for the protective clothing and chemicals, feeling a bit sorry for any European that arrived on these shores having to deal with the stinging little beasts! I have heard that midges in Scotland are nothing to trifle with either, so perhaps Templars would have been prepared!

Mr. Wayne Murphy, an impressive individual, was my armed guide through a wild landscape, with no trails or paths to a hidden site that few have ever set foot in for potentially hundreds of years, other than loggers and the rare hunter.

Wayne Murphy took me past the road on the Reservation named after his family denoting his tie to the past and the land. He is what I would describe as a blond Native American. I could see that his bone structure was Indigenous, but he bore the coloring of his Irish Great Grandfather.

I hoped this would not be taken out of context while writing this, but I could see both Peoples within his physical characteristics. Europe and Native American in equal balance. The perfect representative in search of the last of the Templars in the New World and their Indigenous Allies.

Six
Into the Forest

He told me in a private moment that he struggled with his heritage at times, and felt that he didn't truly fit in anywhere.

Irish immigrants had a tough time in the early days of America, suffering prejudices inherited from England. The Native American struggle has been a path filled with modern uncertainty, tragic historical upheavals, requiring great courage to move forward.

However, there was no mistaking the honed will to live beating within the heart of his family. If the world fell apart, it would be he and his family that would be able to handle living off-grid!

Having stayed with the Murphy's for two weeks, I have a great deal of respect for them and the quiet dignity of my guide. The man who discovered a great secret in the woods. One that is of greater significance than he supposed. As of this writing, I still don't think he realizes what he's found.

Life also revolves around the North Star Casino, which is run by the tribe. We went with his family a few times for meals, chats over a cold beer about the events of the day. One night I tried my hand at a one-armed bandit. I believe I broke even which is rather good considering the house always wins.

I realized the power of the casino for a tribe in the USA as both an income source but also an extensive community center. It was the largest Town Hall I'd ever seen! They were not only employed owners, but had first-rate entertainment and a large stage with a restaurant, and little cafe, gift store, etc.

The Templar Quest
to North America - a Photo Journal

The conference rooms were the perfect location for their meetings where governing issues are resolved. A very powerful resource for the tribe and also the broader community. I was told that people would visit from other nations, including Japan, who had a special love and fascination for the Mohican tribe.

While visiting the Casino one evening, I was introduced to the Vice President, Matthew Putnam. A handsome young man who was instrumental in approving my investigation. Terrie K. Terrio also vouched for my Temporary Use Permit to research and take photographs on the Reservation. It was good to meet Mr. Putnam and to see a younger tribal member choosing to be active in the direction and leadership of his tribe.

Wayne Mary Gretchen

Six
Into the Forest

Wayne Murphy
Tribal Elder of the Mohican Nation Stockbridge—Munsee Band

Seven
The Knight Stone

The Templar Quest
to North America - a Photo Journal

In the months leading up to my arrival in Wisconsin, Wayne spoke of the cross carved onto the large boulder. See photo on previous page. Identifying it as being in the shape of a frog, due to the lichen that had grown over it.

I had to admit that the boulder did indeed bear the resemblance of a frog's head. The green lichen had strategically grown to represent the head, eyes, and mouth.

Having walked into the forest from the logging trail, what he'd called 'frog rock' for many months became slowly visible and growing in size on the approach.

The trees creating a cooling and appreciated canopy overhead, a relief from the heat.

Walking through a forest takes consideration due to bracken, uneven ground, boggy patches, unrelenting mosquitoes that harass every step of the way; coupled with an odd peaceful silence, peppered with the noises of disturbed critters lurking just out of sight.

I felt unduly loud and lacking grace in this environment. I wondered about the Native Americans who lived here during the time Templars would have passed through and what an extraordinary meeting it would have been.

Opposite - George Emanuel Runer - Lord Knight

The Templar Quest
to North America - a Photo Journal

At last the big moment was here -

There was much to take in and understand.

It was clear that the boulder had been left in place by glacier activity from the end of the ice age some 12,000 years ago.

Dropping and carving massive stones as the ice moved south and then receded as it melted.

But it was clear this stone had been touched by skilled human hands. It had been faced, sheered off to receive carvings and to form a shape. Not that of a frog but a human being in armor, a knight.

I could see the intention of a profile wearing what I believed to be a helmet and the beginnings of a shoulder.

It was clear that this carving was never completed.

The Templar Quest
to North America - a Photo Journal

The lack of completion testified that work had been interrupted by an unknown cause. But never the less, I was now confident the Templars had passed through the area and left their mark.

It appeared that a statue of a Templar Knight had been created with a cross on the left shoulder, above the heart.

I was thrilled and oddly subdued at the same time. There was a part of myself that assumed it would be easier to ascertain the carvings on the left shoulder. Rather than being 100% certain, I wanted to vet the carving as was my reputation was on the line.

I've been told that I don't have a poker face. I still assume that I do! My total sympathies for Wayne are needed here as I did not respond to the stone as he'd hoped.

I asked Wayne to take a few photos of myself in front of the Knight Stone to illustrate the profile of what I believed to be an effigy of a Knight Templar.

The Templar Quest
to North America - a Photo Journal

Seven
The Knight Stone

The Templar Quest
to North America - a Photo Journal

Though I could see the outline of the knight, I struggled to find the cross he had photographed. I was very concerned. The cross was pivotal to establishing a solid theory.

I know I must have looked doubtful and could see Wayne become very tense and embarrassed. After all, flying from England was not a small undertaking.

My mind was whirling, reviewing my experiences with carvings in Europe over the past 17 years.

While I was convinced of the effigy carving, I needed better visual data on the cross on the left shoulder as it was very faint.

I needed more time to think and gather myself for the task at hand.

Perhaps the Cave might reveal more information?

Seven
The Knight Stone

Eight
The Cave

Wayne took me to what he termed as 'bear cave' to see three carved crosses inside. It was not far from the Knight Stone and hidden from view as it was down an embankment. A very clever placement. One would have had to know it was there and understood the carvings on the Knight Stone in order to find the cave.

Obviously, the Knight Stone was a marker for the cave.

The cave approach and interior are dangerous and potentially unstable. I will forgo any description of the landscape to conceal its position. However, I can say that at one point, Wayne had gone ahead, turned around and told me step by step where to place my feet and hands so as not to fall or injure myself.

He even suggested how far forward to lean to remain stable. I'm a rather fit person, capable of a decent hike but I very much appreciated the guidance on the approach to the cave.

We had to crawl over the large boulder at the mouth of the cave to gain access to the interior.

I was suddenly aware of the heavy boulders above our heads. It was not a large space. One person could lay comfortably within. We left the cave quickly after having taken a few

Eight
The Cave

photos. No one would have found us if it had collapsed.

I was able to see one of the crosses visibly but struggled to find the other two. However, they did appear in the photos.

Faded ancient carvings are challenging to see as they age, and I have found over the years that lighting and camera resolution can play a large part in visibility.

Inside the cave, Wayne could see the cross through his lens and guided my finger to point towards it with a series of instructions of '...up, right, more right... that's it!'

We clambered back up the hillside to view the surrounds when I had this uncanny and immediate 'hit' that we'd better leave.

It felt as if someone had set a timer and decided we'd seen enough! I felt an impending sense of physical danger wash over me. I did try to keep my voice level and told Wayne that it was time to go. He looked at me and seemed to understand. We left! And quickly...

I am intuitive, we all are, and I had a funny feeling that anyone who was at the site would have received this message loud and chillingly clear.

The Templar Quest
to North America - a Photo Journal

He asked me further once we were away what was going on. I shared with him that I felt an impending sense of physical harm if we stayed. As if we'd broken into someone's home at night and the owner was heading down the stairs with a shotgun. It was time to clear out!

He commented that he could tell by my voice which had raised unbeknownst to myself, so he decided to take me seriously.

Wayne had told me of a few dark legends in the area of restless spirits and their interactions with human beings; they were the stuff of nightmares. I'll let him tell you of these in the future should he decide to do so -

I certainly felt as if I'd been allowed to spend an amount of time at the location but was then asked to leave. Who that was, I am not sure, but I felt as if I'd been emotionally and almost verbally told to clear off post-haste! As if I were trespassing on sacred burial ground. But whose?

Eight
The Cave

The air crackled with energy, an aura of 'extra' that left me with heightened awareness. I've encountered this before having trawled through hundreds of ancient churches and castles in Europe. At times this energy culminated in actual visual contact.

As we visited the location twice, I will save my findings for a later chapter. I'd like to discuss the geography of the Mid-West and the potential alliances of the Templars.

Having clambered through the dense forest and its foliage laden floor, mosquitoes buzzing everywhere, a red tail hawk called out its displeasure of our intrusion. My respect level for Templars on an inland mission was growing.

Nine
Follow the River

But how in the world did Templars manage to get so far inland? The North American coastline is one thing, but Wisconsin?

There is a saying, 'Follow the Money,' in our case, 'Follow the River' -

The Saint Lawrence River is the perfect highway from the North American coastline to Lakes Ontario, Erie, Huron and then to Michigan. Lake Superior, of course, is to the north.

Lake Michigan is the natural stop-over point for a westward mission by Templars.

Mr. Murphy's lost Templar site is due eastward of the Kensington Runestone which was discovered in Alexandria, Minnesota and joins the two together.

It also gives further credence to a Templar visit to Oak Island Nova Scotia, and the outdoor cathedral known as the Nolan Cross.

I traced a known footpath with Google Earth. The waterways would have been used predominantley.

The Templar Quest
to North America - a Photo Journal

But did the Templars travel so far alone?
It is my thought that the answer has to be
a resounding, 'no' -

Ten
Oak Island Carvings

The following information is a brief overview of the stone anomalies found on Oak Island and not meant to be definitive. But to help as an aid to understanding the carvings and structures on the Mohican Reservation, discovered by Wayne Murphy and myself.

Nolan's Cross

It is my fervent thought that the Knights Templar were the originators of Nolan's Cross on Oak Island. The large stones create a cross in the landscape over hundreds of feet.

They had interred sacred treasures on the island as part of their mission in the New and strange World. It was a world of great resources, potential, and danger.

It is probable that Oak Island is a repository of multiple caches from different centuries from the medieval era on up to the American Revolution.

Opposite - Nolan's Cross on Oak Island
Co-ordinates Courtesy of Steven Guptil

The Templar Quest to North America - a Photo Journal

Overton Stone

The carving of the Overton Stone is thought to be a that of a Treaty Stone.

The engraving appears to be a Templar shield, two crossed tobacco leaves, a feather, and a crescent moon.

The carving however is very 'fresh' with defined edges indicating it is not of great age. But placing it on the timeline is difficult. In my estimation it cannot be more than 400 years old.

Is it possible that the creator of the graffiti had knowledge of Templar activities on Oak Island? And carved out the story of a legendary meeting between exiled Templars and the Mi'kmaw tribe, using graphics known only to Templar descendants?

Oral tradition was highly important down the generations to preserve lore and hold it safe for the future.

Strict memorization is the key to underground societies. Symbols convey meaning to those who understand the language of the code.

The Romans remarked on the pride that Druids took to memorize reams of information unlike the conquerors of Britain who were meticulous record keepers.

Opposite - The Overton Stone in Overton, Nova Scotia
Courtesy of Terry J. Deveau

The Templar Quest to North America - a Photo Journal

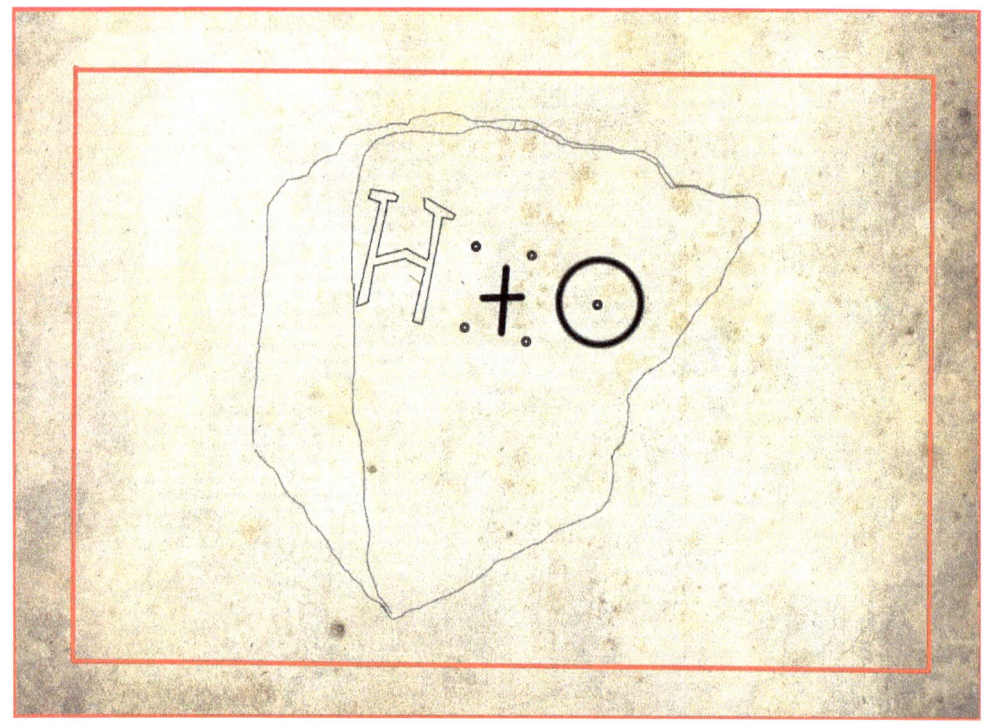

Graphic by Gretchen Cornwall -
Photos of the actual postcard are available online
My image is slightly distorted to protect the original copyright
owner of the vintage postcard.

Ten
Oak Island Carvings

H.O. Stone

Also found on Oak Island are the blasted remains of the H.O. Stone, which in my estimation, is that of genuine Templar symbolism.

It may also have played a role in the location of a Templar treasure vault associated with the Money Pit.

The H.O. Stone is all that remains of a larger boulder with further codes, but it had been blasted to pieces by those who thought wrongly, that there was a treasure beneath.

The H.O. Stone is all that remains of the code.

The Templar Quest to North America - a Photo Journal

New Ross Castle

New Ross Castle has been thought, controversially, to be the remaining foundation stones of a 14th century castle in Nova Scotia, perhaps built by Henry I Sinclair, Earl of Orkney and Lord of Roslin, Scotland.

Alessandra Nadudvari and her husband own the structure and the associated Herm stone. It has been moved to Queens County Museum, Liverpool, Nova Scotia for safekeeping.

I'm so glad that the stone has been taken into a museum for its safety. Weather will no longer erode it and it is now out of danger of being stolen or defaced.

Author, Alessandra Nadudvari, may be contacted through her website:
https://www.adventuresofnicky.com/

I appreciate her permission to publish the photo of the Herm stone as well as her husband Tim Loncarich.

This is only a jot of the evidence found on the island indicating a Templar presence.

The Templars were on Oak Island and ventured westward with the help of their Brave allies.

Opposite-Upper Photo, Courtesy of Alessandra Nadudvari

Opposite-Lower 3D Photo, Courtesy of Doug Crowell

Ten
Oak Island Carvings

Eleven
Brave Allies

The Mi'kmaq Peoples were in the right place in North America to have encountered Vikings as well as Templars.

Their flag has often been remarked upon by many researchers and resembles that of crusader flags. The crescent and the star, motifs mark one as having journeyed to the Holy Land.

The red cross and white background speaks for itself as Templar inspired.

Eleven
Brave Allies

In my estimation, the Mohicans may have also encountered the Templars. Mohicans were originally from the East Coast of the Hudson River valley which is why they are called The People of the Flowing Waters.

I find this poetic as the Cistercian Monks venerated their connection to rivers, streams, and lakes. Some of their abbeys were named after bodies of water.

Kimberly Vele, an eloquent speaker, explains the tribal symbol as a combination of a Christian cross and the many trails that the Mahicans have been forced to take until they were finally settled on the Reservation in Wisconsin.

In 26 minutes, she gives a broad overview of the history of her people and the negative consequences of incoming colonists & wars. It is worth your time:

https://www.pbs.org/video/wpt-documentaries-stockbridge-munsee-mohican-history/

On page 79, you'll see a map of the Mohican Trail of Tears. I find this to be very poignant but also evidence that Templars, centuries ago, could have followed a similar route inland via the water ways. Geography would have created opportunities for the knights to meet their allies.

Indeed, guides for the Templars would have been familiar with trading routes and optimal paths of travel by water or land.

The Templar Quest to North America - a Photo Journal

Flag & Symbols of the Mohican Nation
Stockbridge-Munsee Band

Eleven
Brave Allies

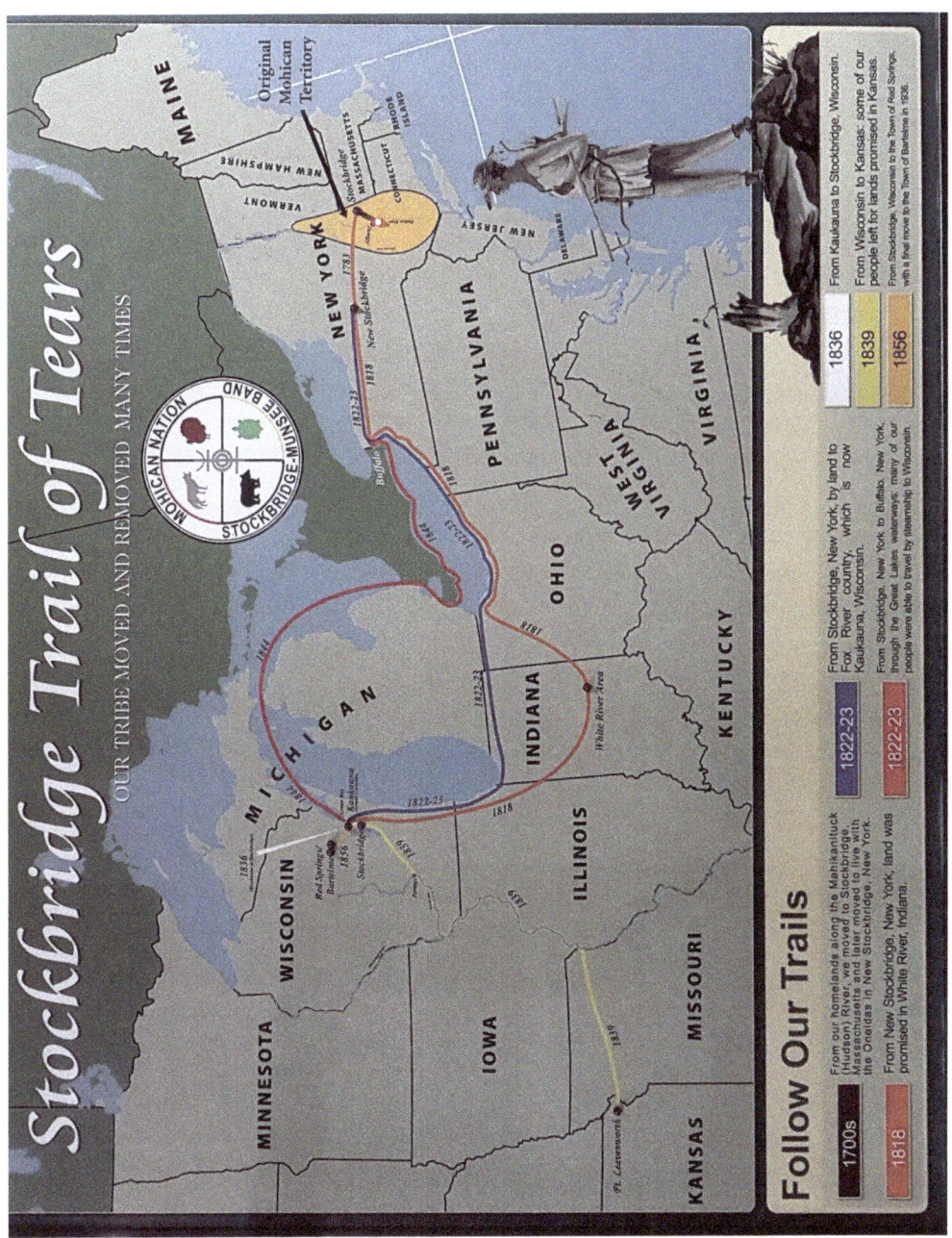

The Templar Quest
to North America - a Photo Journal

During our wait for the rains to subside prior to a second foray to the Knight Stone; we visited the local library where I met Mr. Larry P. Madden, Mahican Language Project Manager for the Stockbridge-Munsee Community, Band of Mohican Indians, Museum.

The Mahicans or Mohicans were of the New York tribes and due west of the Newport Tower in Rhode Island. A key structure thought to have been built by Templars. Duplicating their penchant for round church designs.

The Mohican language and gene pool is rooted in the Eastern Algonquian languages directly on the east coast and perfectly located to have encountered Vikings and Templars.

The Hudson River Valley is a secondary possibility for Templars to have made a westward push other than the St. Lawrence River.

But considering there is evidence to place Templars, Cistercians and of course the Sinclair voyages near Rhode Island's Newport Tower, the multiple voyage theory must be embraced.

The scope of this book does not include an explanation of either the deep history of the Indigenous Peoples of North America or of Templar voyages. As this material has been extensively covered by other historians such as Steven Sora, Dave Brody, Gunn Sinclair and of course one of the father's of the genre, Andrew Sinclair who passed away in spring of 2019.

Eleven
Brave Allies

The focus is a respectful overview with the lens on the discovery by Mr. Murphy and its implications.

Templar voyages, their descendants and precursors the Vikings, would have come across the Mi'kmaqs, Mahicans and the Oneida also known as the People of the Standing Stone which may bear some influence on the discovery of Mr. Murphy's site.

Finally, Templars, perhaps having allied with warriors from the Mi'kmaq, Mahicans or Oneida would have met the Menominee Peoples west of Lake Michigan.

Mr. Madden told me that the Menominee People had been on the land since the Ice Age ended and are also called the Ancient Ones.

The Menominee welcomed the displaced Mahicans (Stockbridge Munsee Band). According to Larry Madden, they were a welcoming, and friendly people since they populated the area at the end of the ice age.

It would be my thought that those Indigenous People travelling with Templars would have been welcomed by the Menominee's.

Twelve
A Day at the Museum

The four sections of the flag of the Mohican People represents the wheel of life. Each season has a cardinal direction & creature ambassador.

Twelve
A Day at the Museum

Mr. Larry P. Madden, Mahican Language Project Manager for the Stockbridge-Munsee Community, Band of Mohican Indians, Museum.

The Templar Quest to North America - a Photo Journal

Mohican Traditional Teachings

Dugout Canoes

In Eastern North America, (Mohican Territory) dugout canoes were typically made from a single log of chestnut or pine. Carefully controlled fires were used to hollow out these logs. The fires were extinguished at intervals to scrape out the burned wood with wood, shell or stone tools, leaving the canoe with a flat bottom and straight sides.

Twelve
A Day at the Museum

Prior Page:

The photo of the Dugout Canoe sign was taken at the museum.

Prior Page:

Gretchen Cornwall at the
Mohican Veteran Memorial

The following two photos were also taken at the Mohican
Veteran Memorial Park

Thirteen
Research

Small museums are a challenge to run, and I've seen many. This one beautifully covered all the bases from lifelike visuals to an audio center with historical overviews read by children.

Outside, the full-size canoe, symbolic garden, though small, and the dwelling was well presented.

While visiting the museum and being guided by the generous Larry Madden, I bought two books for research as well as the desire to contribute towards a well-planned information center. It carried a range of books for purchase as well as a library and archives with numerous portraits of influential and historical representatives of the tribe.

I chose a book on herbal medicine as this skill and craft could save one's life or ease it. Herbal medicine has been embraced with zeal since the 1970's in the USA when the 'green movement' started to gain popularity and understanding. Herbal medicine now cuts across all political and religious barriers.

Having a skilled herbal medicine man or woman in your tribe was a real gift.

Europe also had its own medicine men and women. Abominably, the loss of life, culture, and knowledge was high as countless numbers of them were burned at the stake during the Inquisitions of the medieval era.

Herbal Medical knowledge is power, culture, and sustenance... It is the heady stuff of Identity.

Here is a quote out of the Medicine Generations book I purchased:

Thirteen
Research

"Boneset"

Usage: This is another one of the Medicines that Ella respected the strength of because boneset is a very strong Medicine and should not be used by children. It is good for fever reduction, but only a little should be taken. A tea of the flowers and leaves were used to treat fevers, colds, aching bones and the flu. Dave Besaw recollected that Ella said, "If there is anyone old who wants it, they can go get it and use it for themselves because it is strong enough to cure anything and kill a horse." Granny Gardner and Ella's father liked using boneset, but none of the rest of the family did."

Pg 59. Medicine Generations: Natural Native American Medicines Traditional to the Stockbridge Munsee Band of the Mahicans Indian Tribe by Misty Cook (Davids), M.S. ISBN-13:978-1482779042

Photo taken at the Stockbridge-Munsee Community, Band of Mohican Indians, Museum

The Templar Quest
to North America - a Photo Journal

Wayne's Full-Blood Mohican (Maternal) Great Grandmother had a herbal medicine book that had been well used by his family in decades past.

He described it as having been black with very worn pages containing the handwritten notes and recipes of his Great Grandmother. She sounds like a valued, Wise Woman of the Mohican Peoples. It was not understood till many years later, the value this book represented for his people let alone his direct family. Sadly it was lost at some point as is often the case with family heirlooms, but I hoped that his Great Grandmother would approve of the prior quote.

It has only been the last few decades that the general population base has come to realize that their contribution to history is vast and that history is not just the names and dates of kings, battles, and marriages of the great and wealthy.

The more we know our own past, the greater we understand history, the more likely we can bypass mistakes our ancestors made and make wiser choices for our world.

Also, I purchased 'The Mohican World 1680 to 1750 by Shirley W. Dunn ISBN: 1-930098-12-X'

Aside from being experts with gathering herbs, nuts, and forest fruits, the Mahicans were adepts at using a wild array of plants for weaving, dyes, wearing mostly furs and building semi-permanent structures, they were expert hunters, and the land was bountiful.

In 1640, a Dutch author who came across the Mahicans wrote that the deer were hunted in their thousands and still

Thirteen
Research

The Templar Quest
to North America - a Photo Journal

the population never diminished. Also available were swans, ducks, geese, pigeons, and turkeys. Black bears were prized for their shiny coats and claws for adornment.

"Fish were also a mainstay. The New World, though harsh, was bountiful for those who knew how to gather, hunt, and also farm." Pg 26 and 27 of the book, The Mohican World.

Templars would not have lived a separate life from hunting and fishing themselves; it is only our own modern life that has separated most of us from nature. I am certain they would have benefited from trading and living with Indigenous Peoples.

As to what the relationships might have been, I think they would have been that of curiosity as the numbers of Templars would not have been threatening.

The following quote would have applied to the Templar voyages in North America as it did in the early centuries of colonialism:

"Initial acceptance of European tools, clothes, and weapons was not dictated by need, but rather by desire, convenience, and imitation; it was a social exchange." pg 35

The reason there is not a high amount of domestic waste left by Templars is that their numbers were not high, and anything of value would have been reused endlessly.

A high-quality medieval item found in the collection of a Native American might have been misunderstood as having been brought over by sentimental colonists wealthy enough to have a quality antique knife, sword or perhaps even a buckle, or chain mail. But the Templars did leave dressed stones and carvings.

Fourteen
Mound Builders

Wisconsin state has the largest remaining quantity of burial mounds and effigy mounds than any other state in the union and perhaps the world.

Ancient Indigenous tribes continued to build burial mounds up through 1100 AD, only two decades prior to the creation of the Templar Order in 1119 AD.

Out of the 15,000 to 20,000 mounds, only around 4000 remain due to agricultural activity. Grave robbing and trade in stolen and sacred items have cost the culture a great deal since colonialism.

Early European travellers might have recognized mound building as the Anglo Saxons buried their kings and high ranking elites in a similar fashion.

It was important to myself and also my responsibility as a writer and historian to represent my findings in an ethical manner.

I had to be certain to separate out what I believed to be Templar activity and not confuse it with that of the Indigenous Peoples they encountered. A challenging task.

Fourteen
Mound Builders

Please see the following websites and also a great book on the subject:

Indian Mounds of Wisconsin 30 Nov 2017
by Robert A. Birmingham and Amy L. Rosebrough
ISBN: 13: 978-0299313647

https://madison365.com/exploring-wisconsins-fascinating-native-american-burial-mounds/

http://www.wisconsinmounds.com/

https://www.mohican.com/

I had to understand the lay of the land in order to place the Templars in Wisconsin and to find out who could have aided them or wished to be their allies.

The Last of the Mahicans, the novel by, James Fenimore Cooper, predicted the end of the dignified and original Five Nations tribe.

Fortunately, they still exist and are working to preserve their culture for the future. It was my absolute privilege to have been their guest and given permission to explore their Reservation.

It is my thought that the Templars likewise continued post-1307, meeting the Mahicans, forming alliances with them and other nations, escaping the dark reach of an angry French King with too much power, forcing the Templars underground.

Fifteen
Roche-A-Cri State Park

July 4th found my guide and I heading south to Roche-A-Cri State Park instead of to the local parade and celebrations for Independence Day.

I had a limited amount of time to get to grips with the landscape and its Peoples, let alone the evidence of medieval explorers.

I was very concerned about Cultural Appropriation or Misappropriation and knew the danger of misunderstanding the carvings found on the Mohican Reservation.

It would be folly to ascribe the carvings to the Templars if they were indeed created by the Menominee People.

I did not want to make any announcements of a Templar discovery without comparing the carvings to those of an established site, known to be Indigenous.

The nearest carvings were ninety miles to the south. It was a nerve-racking journey, both Mr. Murphy and I trying to keep our metaphorical cool on approach.

If the carvings were identical in character, it was all over...

I had seen a few carvings from Roche-A-Cri State Park online, but there were only a selected few images. It's what I could *not* see that was preying on my mind.

The park was named after early French explorers and had already been known for a Roche family member by the 1600s. Roche is the root name of the powerful and influential Rochefoucauld family in France who were very close to the crown. The family château was featured on the Curse of Oak Island as their name appeared on Zena Halpern's map.

The Templar Quest to North America - a Photo Journal

Roche is a cousin branch of the Rochefoucald family with many notable individuals throughout history.

When I visited France in 2018 to view the château myself, I was surprised to see the number of times the family name Roche was referenced in the landscape on the way south from the Port of Calais.

Here were Roche family members exploring Wisconsin just 90 miles south of the Templar carvings on the Mohican Reservation!

Cri is a root French word for 'crevice in the rock' and not a derivative of the Native American tribe the Cree.

Fifteen
Roche-A- Cri State Park

The park is large with many hiking trails and terrain that swings from forested paths to 300-foot buttes. It took us a while to find the carvings and ended up at the wrong side of the spectacular park, just off the highway, gazing up at an epic sheer faced monolith created by Mother Nature.

I was, however, appalled by the amount of graffiti and trash everywhere. In fact, I was shocked. I'm not disappointed that I went, but as someone who cares deeply about the preservation of all natural, cultural and historical objects or places, I found myself feeling angry with people who had defaced a striking creation of Mother Nature with spray paint and leaving their crumpled up, empty wrappers all over. I did choose to cut out the offending trash and graffiti as this graceful and majestic site deserved to be remembered as pristine. Pointing the camera upwards hid the refuse of careless people. Thank goodness they could not gain higher ground.

Perhaps the local wardens were overstretched financially as seems to be the case everywhere these days, even in the UK. Austerity has hurt many in all sectors since the multiple economic crashes starting in 2008.

It is a shame that we have to hire others to pick up after ourselves instead of hauling out our own refuse. Taking care of the world is down to each individual and used to be a given in prior generations who took pride in their own stoop, which faced the street.

When did we lose our pride? When did our front door become the province of 'them' or 'they' – to take care of it all?

Looking past the graffiti, I was able to enjoy the monumental scale of the butte.

Fifteen
Roche-A-Cri State Park

We realized we were not in the right place, however, and had to drive back to another area of the park along the highway.

I was not at all sure if we were facing a hike and if so, how far in the July heat. We followed a park road into an information area and decided to keep going through the lovely forest. I realized my blood pressure was up and I felt very adrenalized. This field trip mattered!

To my absolute surprise, the carvings or petroglyphs were just off the road and included a few parking bays! We waited for a small family to leave. The convenience was ridiculous! I honestly thought we were in for a hike. There was certainly no excuse not to enjoy or visit this cultural hotspot.

Opposite: The photo was taken at the wrong location for the petroglyphs, but I was glad to have seen this marvel of nature.

The Templar Quest
to North America - a Photo Journal

I knew in an instant we'd done the right thing by coming down here and missing the July 4th festivities with Wayne's family. I was so grateful as the entire discovery hinged on what we found here at the park.

There was absolutely zero comparison...

The petroglyphs were innocent in comparison to the remains of the bevelled edges of the circle on the cross of the Knight Stone.

I was so relieved...

I've been viewing Medieval graffiti for years across Europe. The petroglyphs of Roche-A-Cri State Park were nothing in resemblance at all.

The soft sandstone at Roche-A-Cri State Park was very easy to carve, versus to the tough granite of the Knight Stone which required skilled hands and fine tools from Europe.

If you find yourself in the area, there is a five-mile trail to the top with views and worth the journey. Our state parks are there for us, We The People - by visiting them and taking ownership, we ensure their historical importance, an inspiring place of beauty to be with family and friends. In mutual Stewardship, we can protect and leave a legacy for the future.

The Templar Quest to North America - a Photo Journal

Above: Close up of a canoe - See detailed opposite photo

Below: The Roche-A-Cri Petroglyphs

Fifteen
Roche-A-Cri State Park

Sixteen
We The People

The Iroquois Confederacy are part of the Six Nations (As described by themselves) and were in contact with Benjamin Franklin. It appears they were inspirational to Franklin in the development of the Constitution of the fledgling Republic that would become the United States of America.

According to Donald A. Grinde, Jr., Ph.D. and Professor of Native American History for the University at Buffalo New York, the Six Nations had no absolute monarch but came together to parley with their opposite number in corresponding tribes.

The phrase 'We The People' the first three words of the Constitution states clearly that power comes from the body of people that make up a nation. Not a monarch with Absolute Rule and placed by God. The concept of the Divine Right of Kings was overturned by the formation of America, a Republic.

'Absolute Monarchists' vs. the concept of 'Meritocracy' was born out of the religious wars and power struggles that tore at Europe for centuries.

'Absolute Power Corrupts Absolutely', is a truth except in rare cases. There may indeed be a benevolent monarch, but the son/daughter may be a different creature altogether. Wreaking havoc upon a kingdom dependent upon empathy and graceful stewardship in governance. Without checks and balances doors open to corruption.

Only a democratic form of governance that represents all peoples can insure against a dictatorship that benefits the few.

If Professor Grinde is correct, the first words from the

Sixteen
We The People

Constitution came directly from the New World and not the Old. Franklin was encouraged in 1754 to establish a peaceful Confederacy in like manner to the Iroquois Six Nations.

A council was elected from each Nation by men and women of the tribes. Women had equality with men and therefore were able to vote. No one on the council had more power than the next as a simple form of checks and balances. Sounds a bit similar to the ethos behind King Arthur's Round Table.

Obviously the scenario is far more complex as Franklin drew inspiration from many sources as well as observation of history and the growing Freemason movement in Europe that had Absolute Monarchists quaking in their crowns. Franklin himself was a Freemason.

After the fall of the Templars, the Absolutist French Monarch, King Philip was dead within a year of the execution of their Grand Master Jacques de Molay in 1314, along with the king's young son Louis X. Pope Clement V also died that year. As his body lay in state, someone set it on fire.

Assassinating an anointed king would not have been taken lightly as the medieval world truly believed that kings were put in place by the divine will of god.

Had underground Templars taken a cautious look at this system and whispered of an alternative path down the corridors of history that were the beginnings of democracy?

After all, Templar Grand Master's were chosen by a complex form of elections which included a college of electors, not too dissimilar to the Electoral College in the USA. The Grand Master was the spiritual, political and military leader of the European wide body for life.

The Templar Quest
to North America - a Photo Journal

Had the concept of elected leaders been picked up by one of the splinter groups that incorporated Templarism into their creed?

If the Templars went underground after Pope Clement V had been illegally elected and used by absolutist monarch, King Philip, they would have elected their own commanders down the centuries as a preventative measure against 'top down' betrayal.

A natural progression of early democratic ideas could have soaked into alternative groups such as the Freemasons the Rosicrucians and trading Guilds.

The terrors of WWI saw many kingdoms replaced by varying forms of democratic governance and some dictatorships.

Britain managed to keep its monarchy but had become a Constitutional Monarchy. A mix of democracy and ancient traditions that had been tempered by the will of the people.

These traditions are deep seated in the Magna Carta of 1215 AD. England had been on the march to a strong legal system for centuries which is one of the reasons why the crown survived the upheavals caused by the French Revolutions.

Eventually, the Iroquois would side with the British, and the Mahicans would side with the Colonists.

The stage was set for the famous novel, The Last of the Mahicans. The Mohawk, fighting alongside the British, harassed the Mohican heroes which led to tragic consequences in the novel.

Seventeen
The Lost Temple in the Woods

Having examined the history of the burial and effigy mound culture of Wisconsin and also that of Roche-A-Cri State Park, I was convinced that the site I had investigated on the Mohican Reservation was indeed that of the Knights Templar, fleeing to North America in the face of persecution and greed.

Perhaps they were on a mission to find Prestor John, a legendary Christian King who might be able to restore their order and the Holy Land? A king whose existence has been chased by many a historian.

They would have been carrying diplomatic correspondence from Bernard de Clairvaux at the dawn of the Order. A mission sanctioned by the Grand Master of the Templars, Hughes de Payens. This is a mission that could have been carried out over decades. It is difficult to pin down the genesis of the Templars in Wisconsin.

*

The first visit to the standing stone in the woods and the cave bore mixed results and had not delivered a 100% wow moment.

I had flown across the Atlantic to see a Templar cross, and it had not been as vivid or apparent as the photos I'd received. Had nature erased the evidence? Was I too late to capture the moment in time?

Wayne was greatly disappointed that it was not a conclusive visit. We spent a great deal of time talking over the events of the our first foray into the woods.

The Templar Quest
to North America - a Photo Journal

I decided to review my photos, thoughts, and experiences of dealing with faint carvings and graffiti in Europe. I hit the books and started to research the history of the area.

Wayne took his wife out for the evening to gain a fresh perspective and shake off the dust of the first exploration to the standing stone. They headed to the North Star Casino.

It was at this stage that I wanted to vet the carving against that of a known Native American site. Our visit to Roche-A-Cri Park was definitive, and my confidence was higher. I had also spent a few days reviewing photos and historical information.

The weather the night before our planned second visit to the site was horrid. Torrential downpours laced with sheet lightning kept me up most of the night with its obnoxious thunder. I was worried about the site and what would be left of it after another extreme weather event.

Typically, I do enjoy a good theatrical storm, but we had work to do the next day and time was running out. Would we be able to see the carvings at their best, or would the carvings be in worse shape due to the storm and heat? What would travel conditions be like? Could we even get to it?

The strikes and sheets of light poured into the room past the blinds and around the blanket I put up over the curtain rail.

The storm had passed in the early morning hours, and sun was predicted for the day. There are some days when coffee isn't enough... But adrenaline helps!

Eighteen
Wisconsin's Templar Castle

Wayne parked on the same old logging road to gain better access to the site he'd discovered as he had on the first trip.

There were a few large boulders just off the road. I asked him about them on our first trip out, and he'd said that they had to be moved by crane to clear the road for logging. However they'd been 'faced' or 'dressed' at some point.

I was beginning to see the boulders differently. It is so easy to walk past one innocuous piece of evidence unless you understand what is in front of you in the broader context of all.

During my journey, I noticed mile upon mile of glacial boulders on the Mohican Reservation and surrounding area. Most had natural gentle curves as they'd been worn away over time by the glaciers tumbling them along and thousands of years of weather-related wear and tear.

As we drove through Wisconsin, I studied the landscape in order to better understand what Wayne had discovered. I was beginning to see a pattern of oddities at his site in particular. The stones found near the Knight Stone and Cave had been dressed for use in a fortification or castle.

Templars and their descendants were in Wisconsin quarrying naturally found boulders and stones for use in building a relay station to resupply outbound and inbound journeys. They were preparing to build a Preceptory on the now Mohican Reservation of Wisconsin!

The Templar Quest
to North America - a Photo Journal

These photos were taken by myself on our second visit to the site. Wayne revisited the site a third time at my behest and took the following. The photos are combined.

Nature does not split rocks with 90-degree angles. Repeatedly and only in one small area. Especially if the boulders are supported by the land and not been cracked due to a lack of earth beneath or a naturally occurring slope which would stress the stone causing it to crack. One crack might divide a stone but not several 90-degree angle cuts in one area diameter, not to be repeated for miles around.

These were medieval quarrying techniques not used by Indigenous Peoples. The only group capable of crossing the Atlantic and with motive, were the Knights Templar.

Eighteen
Wisconsin's Templar Castle

The Templar Quest to North America - a Photo Journal

Eighteen
Wisconsin's Templar Castle

Nineteen
The Triangle of the Knight Stone

The ground was sodden from the night before, and the forest appeared to have changed in the night with fallen branches and leaves. The high winds seemed to have shifted the terrain from the prior visit, and all appeared new to me.

Wayne and I were tense and had prepared for the new photoshoot having spoken at great length of every angle and potential we could think of –

Upon seeing the Knight Stone again, I was convinced that it represented a European warrior in armor.
As we approached the standing stone,
Wayne said a profound prayer to 'open our eyes'...

The torrential rain and cloud cover gave a totally different view and experience in opposition to our prior visit. It did, indeed open our eyes. It felt as if the whole exploration of my journey had a guiding hand behind it and that the weather had been orchestrated to our benefit.

Water had saturated and highlighted the stone for us to see with greater clarity the secrets of its past. The mood had totally changed.

The Templar Quest
to North America - a Photo Journal

There was not just one cross, but a few, along with medieval coins often used in the heraldry of the flag of the Languedoc in Southern France and the Kings of Jerusalem.

Both Wayne and I felt blessed to have been given the right lighting conditions necessary to see the crosses. The storm had drenched the Knight Stone, making it possible to see the ancient carved motifs.

Simply pouring a bottle of water over it would not have given the same result. This technique is often helpful when researching medieval carvings, the amount of water needed could not have been carried by us into the woods in order to produce the right lighting results; coupled with the overcast conditions. We'd been given a second opportunity to find the Templars.

The Triangle

The Knight Stone was a good-sized boulder, and I wanted to see if the lichen might be hiding any other carvings. I gently peeled back the lichen from the right side of the boulder. It came off easily.

The Templar Quest
to North America - a Photo Journal

- Disclaimer -

I don't recommend that anyone attempt the removal of lichen from either old gravestones or potential historical monuments as the roots can dig into the stone and damage it if it is carelessly pulled off. The best approach for lichen removal is non-toxic and approved gravestone cleaning chemicals available online. Since I have experience with old monuments I knew how to proceed.

Having gently tested a small corner, I knew that the granite would not come away with the lichen. It was a good inch thick, indicating great age and peeled off easily.

Lichen has a slow growth rate, most varieties only manage less than a millimetre a year. As this was an inch thick, I knew it was very old with a blackened and dark underlay. If there were other carvings, it was difficult to find them.

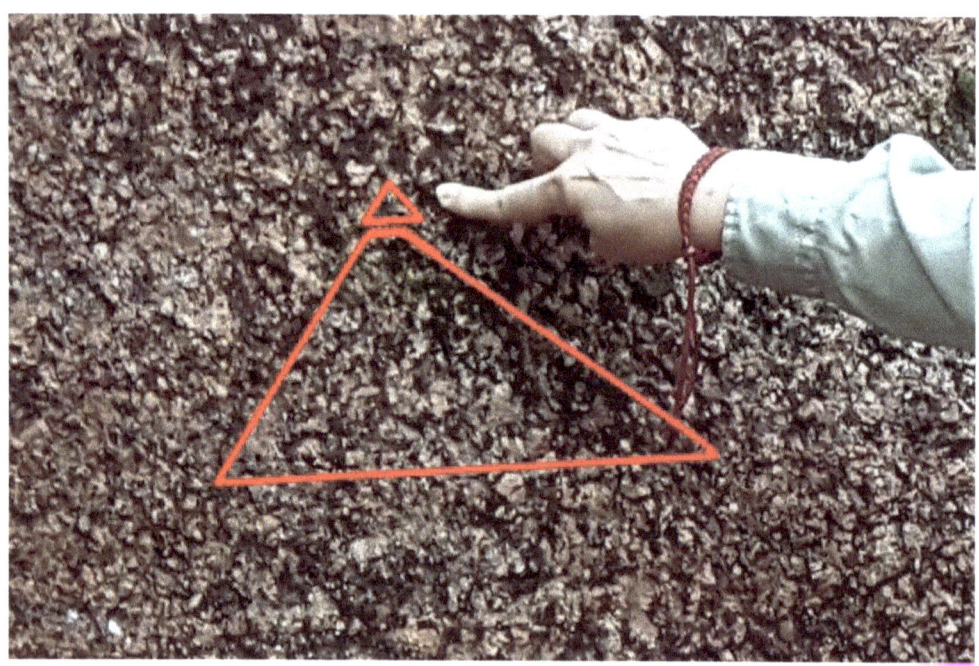

Nineteen
The Triangle of the Knight Stone

I was not disappointed. The carving is raised up, not indented. The surrounding area around the carving had to have been flattened to achieve the raised bevelled edges.

The oddity here is that of the floating capstone, a unique design familiar to many Freemasons and can be found on the reverse side of the dollar bill. This is a symbol that post dates the Templars, yet here it is on the Knight Stone.

Could the floating cap stone above the pyramid symbolize the survival of the Templar Order after it had been cut off? Knights Templar 2.0 a new pyramid emerges?

The Eye of Providence is also on the reverse of the Great Seal of the United States approved in 1787, but where did it come from in a medieval context?

The Templar Quest
to North America - a Photo Journal

There is a precedence of the use of the Obelisk in Europe, left by ancient Rome, Egypt and also in the Axumite Kingdom of Ethiopia which is tied in with the legendary King Prestor John.

The Obelisk is an elongated pyramid, in essence. A long column capped with a smaller pyramid.

The Obélisque d'Arles in France is a 4th century Roman Obelisk. The Templars had a Preceptory in Arles which was an important port.

You may enjoy reading about the city and seeing photos of the obelisk here:

https://en.wikipedia.org/wiki/Ob%C3%A9lisque_d%27Arles

The blue is a reminder of the sky or heavens and the eye set in gold, the metal of the sun, a symbol of eternal accountability and protection. The triangle is always representative of geometry and an enlightened state of mind through life-long learning and endeavour.

Nineteen
The Triangle of the Knight Stone

The Tetragrammaton is a complex sacred image containing the biblical name of God in Hebrew, dating back thousands of years.

The image below was taken at the Palace of Versailles, France, by P. Vasilliadis, at the 5th Chapel.

The Templar Quest
to North America - a Photo Journal

The language of symbols in most cultures arises out of a need to explain a thousand words in one graphic or perhaps a stained glass window. Most people did not read and an agreed language of symbols rose out of the need to explain in quick terms, entire concepts.

The majority of Europeans were illiterate and did not speak Latin. One was expected to go to mass but that did not mean you would understand what was being said. The basic stories were known and told in pictorial form in churches that served as books in stone.

The Templars were engaged in church and cathedral building. Depending on the wealth of the particular site, they ranged from great simplicity to the high use of stained glass windows or murals.

A common design feature in Templar churches is either the eight sided tower, a symbol of infinity, or a round tower with the same implications.

The Tetragrammaton on the prior page is set within the sphere of all creation, the light of the eternal sun. A similar message as the eight sided tower or round tower of the Templars. All encompassing and never ending, with the life giving gold of the sun of the creator.

Twenty
The Knight Stone Reveals Itself

I took the below photo at the Templar church of Saint Mary's in Radnage, High Wycombe, England. Recent conservation work revealed medieval wall murals. The faint outline of a Cross Pattée can still be seen today -

The Templar Quest
to North America - a Photo Journal

Understanding the carvings on the Knight Stone is challenging due to the amount of erosion. The picture is not complete.

It may be that this monument is of equal importance to the Westford Knight carved slab in Westford Massachusetts.

Examining Wayne's monument on site and close up photography, patterns emerged that had gaps missing but it was clear what the design was meant to be -

The original Templar Cross pattée that Wayne had discovered was towards the middle of the monument and should have been on or near the left shoulder.

I do think this indicates a larger pattern of graffiti that has not survived the test of time. Why would a Templar cross be towards the bottom of the monument? It was telling a story that we may never know the full extent of -

The lost information may speak of other locations nearby and star alignments that marked holy days.

Bringing the photos home to England, pouring over them at length, tossed up a surprise-

A Templar Knight shield-

I was shocked! Wayne and I could not see the whole carving in person, but there it was in the photos!

Why was the shield so small in comparison to the rest of the structure? Since the Knight Stone is almost full height this indicates that there were other carvings on the stone which we cannot see today. Perhaps as time goes on, more will become available to us with leaps in technology.

The Templar Quest
to North America - a Photo Journal

I had not really expected something of this nature but hoped that there was more to the Knight Stone than we first thought.

The double circle around the equal lateral cross is filled with Annulets which are a heraldry symbol in use during the Middle Ages.

Templars were not permitted to use heraldry devices. So, who does this heraldic symbol represent?

At this time I do not have an answer, but there were noble houses who used the Annulet that were involved in the Holy Land.

If this monument does represent a fallen knight, could he have been a lay brother? A nobleman who was on a mission with the Templars, but so well respected that he was memorialised with the symbol for his family line rather than the anonymity of a initiated Templar priest? In this case, both appear to be embraced.

One could join the Templars for two years and return to your prior life which could even include wives, children and wealth. This does toss up the question, Who were the Templars?

The Kite shield was used from the 10th century up to the mid 12th century, however, there does seem to be an argument that the shield was in use for a few hundred more years though with reducing frequency.

Twenty
The Knight Stone Reveals Itself

The image of the Kite Shield on page 131 contains nine remaining Annulet coins. It appears there is room for a further 21 coins.

In traditional medieval iconography, Templar shields are sometimes shown with 30 'dots' or 'pellets' as rivets. However the rivets represent the 30 pieces of silver given to Judas for the betrayal of Jesus.

Though they may be actual rivet placements, it is still relevant that they number in 30 total.

Alessandra Nadudvari shared this concept with me via email, after she'd read my first edition. I chose to include it in the 2nd edition with the new cover.

The statue in Tomar Portugal of the influential Templar Master, Gualdim Pais, includes a shield very similar to the one in the above illustration.

The Templars backed Afonso, nephew of Bernard de Clairvaux, in his battle with Moorish Spain, carving out the kingdom of Portugal and crowning him. Port-U-Grail had become a Templar kingdom along with Switzerland.

Here is the direct quote Alessandra sent:

"Afonso, commemorated the event by amending the shield of Portugal he carried with him from his late father - the blue cross over a shield of white - to incorporate thirty silver bezants, a reminder of the symbolic entry requirement into the Templar order."

Freddy Silva: First Templar Nation, pg. 118

The Templar Quest
to North America - a Photo Journal

Twenty
The Knight Stone Reveals Itself

Please note the placement of the Kite Shield used by Templars on the opposite photo of the Knight Stone

Also the Templar cross shown in full in prior photos towards the middle of the structure.

As the Templar Castle was never completed, is it possible that the carving meant for the Knight Stone was also left unfinished? Did the encampment fall prey to a terrible disaster?

The Knight Stone deserves to be examined further, but for now, I must put this project to bed –

Twenty One
The Templar Tomb

The light was starting to fade and we did not want to get caught in a dark forest or cave. We both felt we had to leave our exploration of the Knight Stone, leaving two sides unexplored.

Having felt lifted by our success, we then made our way to the cave.

By this time, I was convinced that the cave was indeed man-made.

Having used the term 'boulder' with the Knight Stone the man-made cave, by contrast, had been created out of a behemoth of a rock of epic proportions. It was a mountain of solid stone, but it had been cracked and carved by expert hands for a sacred duty.

The massive boulder had been cleaved and split in order to create a pie shape that could be separated from the remaining boulder. This allowed for right-angle walls and an easier method than having gouged out the cave without disturbing a natural roofline. The architects wanted to have flush right angle walls. The only way to achieve this with any speed was to have cracked it open into the pie shape. After all, they had a fortified tower to build.

As this was easier the cave now had two entrances rather than one - the larger ceremonial entrance and the smaller passage that may have been an exit used after having dragged a coffin within the main entrance. Both entrances would have been blocked by large fitted stones.

Twenty One
The Templar Tomb

Wayne had known of the cave for forty years, and it had at one point been wide enough to walk into it from the side entrance though clearly smaller than the main entrance.

The side entrance is so tight that only a gap now exists, this being due to the slippage of the main original mother boulder having slid down the hillside a few feet over decades of erosion.

This is one reason that it is such a dangerous site as the original configuration has changed over hundreds of years. With the amount of rain fall the night before and a very sodden ground, collapse was possible. We had to be careful.

In order to create a roof, smaller boulders were lifted above the open-air space created by the pie shape. The roofline boulders had been notched by human hands so that they would retain their place above. It reminded me of a comma used in punctuation to stabilize the 'round' boulders.

Wayne and I were grateful for this, of course, as both of us needed to be within for our investigation.

The roof boulders had shifted as well, however, and we were hoping that further slippage would not have happened due to soggy ground from the storm of the night before. In retrospect, both of us going within was careless.

He had for the 2nd time, left his keys in the gas/petrol tank alcove behind the flap. He told me that if anything happened to him that I was to leave him there and go get help. He was armed for the 2nd trip as well, but if the earth moved due to the deluge of the night before, we were both in trouble.

Twenty One
The Templar Tomb

The boulder we had to climb over had once been on the roof. It had fallen down over time. There was also a rough triangle stone that sat to one side of the mouth of the cave on the left.

Wayne surmised correctly that it had been a decorative triangle on one side of the boulder we had just had to climb over and that it had a partner off to the right of it. But that all three pieces had slid off the roof over time.

The Templar Quest
to North America - a Photo Journal

The circular stone in the above photo would have sat behind the stone that Wayne and I had to climb over. It is notched on the lower right side, hidden behind the fern. It is elongated, almost like a stout log backed up by another like stone.

It appears that it had been faced and may include a design pattern on it. The bald spot was cleared by Wayne and revealed a 'coin' that has been 'punched' -

There are often little messages and sculptures in Europe hidden behind other supporting stones, never meant to be seen but only by the Creator. A humble gift or message hidden from human eyes but there in secret for God.

Twenty One
The Templar Tomb

The shape is an Annulet or Punched Coin in Medieval heraldry. It can indicate either a high ranking priest such as a Templar Commander or a fifth son.

Annulets were used on coins minted in Jerusalem under the Kings Baldwin, II, III and IV -
See below image

   The denier is a Crusader coin and is emblazoned on one side with a Templar cross. Note the Annulets which create a cross on the left top side.

   Since the carving exists on the Tomb and the Knight Stone, the site is Templar with a link to Jerusalem. Or the individual who may have been interred here, could have been from a noble house who used the emblem in their coat of arms.

   Is this a message that the site in the New World has been infused with that of the symbols of Jerusalem and in so doing, the Templar Preceptory in Wisconsin is an extension of Oak Island the New Jerusalem?

Coin found on NumisBids.com

Münzen & Medallion GmbH
Auction 47 23 May 2019

The Templar Quest
to North America - a Photo Journal

Standing on top of the tomb. Note the long curved roof stone by my shoulder and the right angled wall of the entry way

Twenty One
The Templar Tomb

Is there a deliberate attempt on the part of the architect and stone masons to produce the tomb of Christ?

The roof line comprises of round stones that may be metaphorically 'rolled' away on the third day -

The Templar Quest to North America - a Photo Journal

Twenty One
The Templar Tomb

The opposite photos were taken from the gap on the side of the tomb. Wayne told me that years ago when he was hunting in the woods, he could walk through this gap into the cave if he turned sideways.

The symbol of the fish next to that of an upside down triangle is very interesting. Is this a mirror of the capped pyramid on the Knight Stone? Only in reverse?

Considering the triangle carving on Oak Island, I wonder if there is a relationship?

The Templar Quest
to North America - a Photo Journal

Wayne found a bear track near the site -
I'm glad that we did not meet up!

Inside the Templar Tomb, standing next to the narrow gap
Opposite

Small cross on back wall at head height. Three in total –

Opposite page – Inside the Tomb looking back at the main entrance

Twenty One
The Templar Tomb

My finger on the opposite page is on the lower cross shown on this page with white arrows

Do the crosses represent the night sky or directions?

Why are there two in a vertical line while a third is off to the side? It appears to be a Right Angle Triangle.

Wayne thought it might represent the three crosses of the crucifixion.

The Templar Quest to North America - a Photo Journal

Prior page - Inside the Tomb looking back at the main entrance

Granite, simply put, is composed of potassium feldspar which creates a matrix for quartz to develop.

Some granite types are a natural source of uranium from 10 to 20 parts per million in contrast to other types of rock at 1 to 5 ppm. It has been debated whether granite may be used for kitchen counters due to its high radiation emission. However it has not been proven to be an issue except in cellars or underground rooms without ventilation.

Quartz is used for its electric potential when 'vibrated mechanically'. Quartz has found long standing value in watches and crystal oscillator circuits that can create an electrical signal with a precise frequency, also generating a voltage.

Ancient and great architecture from antiquity, such as Egypt and India have built religious structures containing high contents of granite in order to produce heightened awareness during ceremonies due to the resonance of the quartz.

Is it possible the Templars learned of these architectural effects on the human brain during their time in the Middle East and their secret travels in the far orient? As quartz is prone to resonate when vibrated how would it respond to sacred chanting or the haunting and beautiful sounds of Gregorian Chants? Would it create a feed-back loop between priest and sacred chamber, inducing a state of awareness where prayer and secret initiation methods bestow greater lasting blessings on the celebrants?

Inside the Templar Tomb with the sword and cross

The Templar Quest to North America - a Photo Journal

Twenty One
The Templar Tomb

The motif to the right is that of the Brothers of the Sword that merged with the Germanic Teutonic Order and became known as the Linovian Order. The German warrior monks were known to have connected with the Templars.

I have shared this with you in order to illustrate the sword and the cross in the prayer position in the opposite photo.

The Linovian Order has chosen to separate the cross and the sword.

The sword in the Templar Tomb to the left might be Germanic in descent as the Templars drew their members from across Europe. It's a possibility -

The cross has been sharply cut into the granite, some edges are more eroded than others. I do think that a blade is apparent but there has been a constant drip pouring down the inside of the cave at this juncture where the blade has been carved, wearing the blade out in places.

The sword is on the upper left side of the wall of the tomb near the gap. Ceremonial in purpose or a literal tomb?

The Templar Quest
to North America - a Photo Journal

Having penetrated so far west and taking on board that there would have been an alliance with the local Menominee, participating Mi'kmaq, Oneida and or Mohican guides, the first order of business is survival.

Food sources were everywhere, but shelter would also be important. My thought is that Templars would have initially brought their own tents as this was a European technique for the field of battle. It may be that as time progressed that Templars could have adopted the sturdy, warm huts built by the North American tribes.

It was clear that quarrying and dressing stones had taken place but the creation of a time-consuming tomb was interesting.

I have examined other chambers built by Indigenous Peoples, but Wayne's discovery is a very different nature to the other examples on the Eastern Seaboard. I believe Wayne's cave to be of European construction.

If this location on the Mohican Reservation was strategic for a Westward push, in this case towards Minnesota where the Kensington Runestone was carved, building a fortified tower would have been key to survival. Or at least a comforting reminder of home. After all, the Templars were famous for being great engineers, architects with an almost obsessive drive to build in stone.

Taking time out from building a tower to create a tomb is curious as most Templars would have been interred with a grave slab over the top of a stone coffin. Adorned with only a simple sword as a marker and perhaps a staff with a compass rose.

Twenty One
The Templar Tomb

The name of most interred knights was not included, as all was given up to service to God including ones name. In rare cases church records have survived and the name of the Templar had been logged.

In contrast to Templar burial practice, is that of the Westford Knight which is festooned with codes, stars and a knight in full 14th century armor.

The man now known as the Westford Knight whose name is not marked on the intricate grave slab, had been apparently sailing to the New World with Henry I Sinclair, Lord of Roslin and Earl of Orkney.

Lord Sinclair's grandson, William, built Rosslyn Chapel in Scotland as a tribute to mark the voyage. The Westford Knight stone gave full honors to the fallen nobleman, but the grave slab was also an opportunity to leave codes for future adventurers to the area.

The cave Wayne discovered, was just as elaborate an undertaking as the Westford Knight's grave. The act of cutting the stone into a roofless chamber was massive along with the marker, the Knight Stone, whose carvings were intriguing in their detail.

Was the tomb intended for a single man? If so, his remains and any signs of a coffin disappeared centuries ago. Wayne is convinced it is a tomb of a well-respected Templar officer and leader. He may be right.

If it had been used as a burial of a Templar commander whose coffin was robbed, what happened to his remains and why would they have taken the coffin?

Twenty One
The Templar Tomb

More than likely remains were carried off by scavengers or perhaps reburied as a mark of human kindness by unknown individuals.

Grave robbing was rife in Native American burials and is a crime today. The same unscrupulous robbers during the post-colonial era would have hit the jackpot with a Templar grave, choosing to sell off any items that he'd been buried with -

I myself think it is also possible that the small cave is ceremonial and was to play a large part in Templar initiation ceremonies in the New Jerusalem. It was therefore central to the preceptory to have a sequestered Initiation & Prayer Chamber on site.

Templars in Britain had multiple caves where secret meditation and prayer practices were maintained. These often took place outside of a tower fortress or castle.

Royston Cave is just underneath the crossroads of the town of Royston where Templars had a preceptory eight miles away at the town of Baldock. This is but one example of the underground world of the Templars in Europe.

The Tomb found by Wayne may have been their first task in creating their outpost in the wilds of North America. Their religious beliefs taking center stage once the needs of survival had been tended to.

Having the capacity to pray undisturbed just outside the main living site was obviously a high priority, having been established as a practice in Britain and in the underground maze of tunnels under Temple Mount in Jerusalem.

The Templar Quest
to North America - a Photo Journal

Once the Templar Initiation Chamber had been created, preparing stones left strewn about by glacier activity, was the next step.

Establishing a fortified tower was important in case the political situation with the local tribes was disturbed, perhaps by an outside tribe wishing to gain the resources of the rich area?

Twenty Two
The Wisconsin Templar Preceptory

The Wisconsin Preceptory would have been a relay post for travel between the North East Coast and the Great Lakes.

The Templar Cave and Knight Stone are due east of the Kensington Rune Stone in Minnesota. The newly discovered site verifies Viking and Knight Templar settlements on Oak Island Nova Scotia and is a link in a chain heading west.

It is possible that Templars visiting North America were on a mission to find Prester John, a fabled Christian King of great wisdom and wealth.

Bernard de Clairvaux, a main mastermind behind the Templars, sent men out on secret missions to find and entreat the mysterious king for help in securing the Holy Land.

It is my thought that Prestor John may have been a king out of Ethiopia, one of the earliest Christian kingdoms in Africa. Since the kingdom was surrounded by Muslim countries, getting to Ethiopia would have been almost impossible.

The Templars may have been trying to find the country by another route. Eventually, Templars did find their way to Ethiopia as the many churches built out of solid stone have their architectural traits.

The benefits of being in North America also provided resources such as gold which was plentiful just north of Oak Island in Gold River.

The Templar Quest
to North America - a Photo Journal

Zena Halpern discovered the possibility of Gold River as to why the Vikings and Templars who followed, were drawn to the dangerous world of untamed North America.

Oak Island may have been considered a sacred site to Templars. Nolan's Cross is a symbol that Oak Island was the landing site of the New Jerusalem.

The coconut or coir fibres found on the island and carbon-dated to 1200 AD via five different tests, can only mean one thing. The Knights Templar had infused the sacred aspects of the palm into the fabric of Oak Island.

Please visit the following website:
http://www.oakislandtreasure.co.uk/research-documents/discoveries/coconut-fibre/

The coconut fibres are not native to North America but were an import. What were they doing on Oak Island and where did the Templars find them? Had they been cultivated in the Holy Land? Coir fibres were written of by Arab Scholars in the 10th century. The tropical coconut was not unknown in the desert regions of the Mediterranean but did not naturally grow there due to the high amount of humidity and water needed. The date palm however was native to the middle east.

Since Templars were great navigators it's possible they took coconuts with them as a food source regardless of their origin & potential exotic voyages. It makes sense to this researcher that they had cultivated Oak Island as a New Jerusalem just off a coastline where they'd hoped to build a series of preceptories just as they had across Europe and the Middle East.

The symbolism of the palm is a nod to Palm Sunday and the triumphal entry into Jerusalem by King Jesus.

Twenty Two
The Wisconsin Templar Preceptory

Carbon dating is a difficult science and it is important to state that future results may throw my theory of the coir fibres having been planted by Templars, into question. It is important to be able to shift ones theory with new evidence, as long as the new evidence has been interpreted correctly.

However, new evidence came to light on The Curse of Oak Island. Geoscientist Dr. Ian Spooner was brought in to assess the swamp during Season 7 and has so far been in 7 episodes including a Drilling Down Special.

He took a core sample of the swamp. The organic material at the lower level dated it to 1220 AD! In other words human hands had interfered with the so called swamp during the same time period as that of the coconut fibres. Evidence that the Templars had created the swamp and were on the island in the 13th century is stacking up!

I in turn was able to verify the lost gem on the Mohican Reservation as that of a Templar settlement and not just that of a lone random cross, carved in an unknown decade by simple passers-by.

No, this was that of a military mission, the archaeological remains of a suppressed order of knights out of Europe!

The Last of the Templars had crossed the Atlantic to meet and become allies to proud Indigenous Peoples, some of them would surely have been the Last of the Mohicans.

Wisconsin has a rich and ancient culture that now has a new chapter which includes the Knights Templar.

Twenty Three
Homeward Bound

The last day of my investigation into the forest of Wisconsin & the Templar Castle. Weary but inspired, it was time to go home and start writing.

Thank you Chelsea Murphy for your company and the photo of myself, Wayne and Mary.

Twenty Three
Homeward Bound

Wayne, his wife Mary and daughter in law Chelsea, took me to the Milwaukee Airport. It was an enjoyable drive.

The three hour journey gave us a chance to stop a few times and over indulge in celebratory junk food. I was initiated into the wonders of the fantastic Wisconsin cheese curd.

Final Thoughts & Deep Conversations

I had the privilege of getting to know Wayne and his family. He and I spent a great deal of time talking about the challenges of his home state of Wisconsin, outside of the research on the Templar site he'd discovered. Not to bring this up seemed to cut out a whole chapter from my journey.

It is a risk for an author to speak about topics outside the remit of their book. However I could see how the economy was hurting the state of Wisconsin.

Dairy is a main economic staple of Wisconsin farming and a huge producer of cheese for the nation. As I write this, I am aware of the growing vegan movement and the era of political correctness and its equal opposite backlash. We live in challenging and uncertain times... I've never seen so many homeless in the USA, it's shocking & unacceptable. Life is harder as opportunities shrink for all of us.

I believe that we must respect each other, on all sides of the fence. As a woman, I too have faced behavior I should not have had to deal with...

I also find it inexcusable on any one given day to see the levels of vitriol spewed out on social media and elsewhere. It is highly disturbing and upsetting. Surely we can do better?

The Templar Quest
to North America - a Photo Journal

A huge part of Wisconsin is dependant on its agricultural heritage. Peoples lives who need to pay their mortgage and feed their families are at risk and have been since the economic crash of 2008. Small independent family farms have been bought up by larger corporate entities. Adding to this pressure? The future of the planet.

How we will all decide to live in the future should be handled with thought for the economic needs of those dependant on our food chain and infrastructures.

Conservative Prime Minister, Margaret Thatcher, of the United Kingdom, shut coal mines down without thought as to how the communities affected would be able to handle the transition. She chose to take Great Britain into the service & financial industries instead.

The consequences had a terrible knock on effect for towns in the UK created to support local mines. Once mines shut down, entire towns became unemployed from shop keepers, restaurants etc... Banks repossessed homes... For each one job in a mine or steel mill, seven jobs are lost in town.

Since the 1980's many of these towns have never bounced back and many are generational dependant on welfare as sufficient retraining had not been offered at the outset. Improvement is happening, but we lost an entire generation to economic deprivation and the psychological heartache of the loss of personal dignity.

With Climate Change on everyone's mind today, I hope that the political choices of the future are made with compassion, out of the box & creative thinking. We need to take everyone into the future with us. Not just the few who gain in times of a bull market or bear.

Regardless of where you stand on Climate Change, littering in your own back yard is not the way forward. I think that can be accepted by all sides.

Twenty Three
Homeward Bound

It only makes sense to leverage green energy.

Likewise, we do need to think about the future but also transition so that we do not leave whole towns without a future which has been happening in the USA since the crash of 2008. We need a huge shift in our infrastructures.

I hesitated to show the photo of the defaced natural wonder that is Roche-A-Cri State Park, I will show it here as it seems that so much respect has been lost for our surroundings, whether it be at governmental levels, corporate or individual.

The Templar Quest
to North America - a Photo Journal

I could not publish the book without sharing this sad photo of the park as it kept preying on my mind. The amount of litter left at the sacred wonder, spoke of a level of entitlement and ignorance that is endemic.

On all sides of the political fence, I believe we can and should do better, for each other and the world we gift as a legacy to the future embodied by grandchildren.

The passion on all sides speaks of a desire to do the right thing, how we go about it does matter for us all. Top down professional leadership without dehumanizing name calling is needed immediately.

>We are all brothers and sisters under a glorious
>star filled sky by night and a shining sun by day.

There are so many intelligent, well meaning, caring people out there, all trying to do the right thing by their families and communities, regardless of religion and politics.

Amongst the difficulties I do see a high level of care and a drive to serve others on both sides, Republican or Democrat in the USA...
>The concept of Chivalry is as important today
>as it was in the Middle Ages.

The symbol for the town of Magdeburg Germany

How can we take this forward? Be ye male or female - What type of Knight are you?

Are you a Protector? Or a Predator?

Might is Right? Or Might for Right?

Twenty Three
Homeward Bound

Twenty Four
A Special Thank You

I am grateful to have met George Emanuel Runer, Lord Knight, via the wonders of social media. He has brought the Knights Templar into the present with his honed skills.

Sir George is a Re-enactor and educator for medieval fayres of the Northeastern United States. He has taught Gnostic traditions associated with the Knights Templar in Southeastern United States. See respective opposite photos. Sir George is presently based in Pennsylvania and may be found on Facebook. He is also an actor & may be the right knight for your event.

I have not yet met him but he is now a friend thanks to our collaboration on this project. His background as an English teacher has been of great service in editing this work.

I am certain that the last Grand Master would be proud that his Order is portrayed with such heart today by Lord Knight George E. Runer.

Selected Bibliography

Beamon, Sylvia P., and M.A. *Royston Cave - Used by Saints or Sinners?* 1st edition. The Temple Publications, 2008.

Brody, David S. *Cabal of The Westford Knight: Templars at the Newport Tower*. Martin & Lawrence Press, 2009

Butler, Alan. *The Knights Templar: Their History and Myths Revealed*. Reprint edition. New York: Shelter Harbor Press, 2014.

Cook, Mrs Misty D. *Medicine Generations: Natural Native American Medicines Traditional to the Stockbridge-Munsee Band of Mohicans Tribe*. United States: CreateSpace Independent Publishing Platform, 2013.

IMDb. 'Donald A. Grinde Jr.' http://www.imdb.com/name/nm5894980/.

Dunn, Shirley W. *The Mohican World, 1680-1750*. Fleischmanns, N.Y: Purple Mountain Pr Ltd, 2000.

History TV. 'Episode Guide'. https://www.history.co.uk/shows/buried/articles/buried-episodes.

Halpern, Zena. *The Templar Mission to Oak Island and Beyond: Search for Ancient Secrets: The Shocking Revelations of a 12th Century Manuscript*. CreateSpace Independent Publishing Platform, 2017.

Selected Bibliography

Houldcroft, P. T. *A Medieval Mystery At The Crossroads*. Royston: Royston & District Local History Society, 2008.

http://www.wisconsinmounds.com/.

Jones, Dan. *The Templars*. Reprint edition. London: Head of Zeus, 2018.

Markale, Jean. *The Church of Mary Magdalene: The Sacred Feminine and the Treasure of Rennes-Le-Chateau: The Sacred Feminine and the Treasures of Rennes-Le-Chateau*. 1st Ed. Rochester, Vt: Inner Traditions Bear and Company, 2004.

Rosebrough (author), Robert A. Birmingham|Amy L. *Indian Mounds of Wisconsin*. 2nd ed. edition. Madison, Wisconsin: The University of Wisconsin Press, 2017.

Schwartz, Diane. 'Exploring Wisconsin's Fascinating Native American Burial Mounds'. *Madison365* (blog). https://madison365.com/exploring-wisconsins-fascinating-native-american-burial-mounds/.

Silverberg, Robert. *The Realm of Prester John*. New edition edition. London: W&N, 2001.

Sinclair, Andrew. *Rosslyn: The Story of Rosslyn Chapel and the True Story behind the Da Vinci Code*. Illustrated edition edition. Edinburgh: Birlinn Ltd, 2005.

The Templar Quest
to North America - a Photo Journal

The Secret Scroll. First Edition edition. London: Sinclair-Stevenson, 2001.

Sora, Steven. *Lost Treasure of the Knights Templar: Solving the Oak Island Mystery*. Rochester, Vt: Destiny Books,U.S., 1999.

'Stockbridge-Munsee Band of Mohican Indians'. https://www.mohican.com/.

Stockbridge-Munsee Mohican History | Tribal Histories. https://www.pbs.org/video/wpt-documentaries-stockbridge-munsee-mohican-history/.

History TV. 'The Curse of Oak Island'. https://www.history.co.uk/shows/the-curse-of-oak-island.

The Oak Island Compendium. 'The Oak Island Compendium - A Resource for Research and Facts Surrounding the Treasure Hunt at Oak Island, Nova Scotia'. http://www.oakislandcompendium.ca/.

Wolter, Scott F. *The Hooked X: Key to the Secret History of North America*. St. Cloud, Minn: North Star Press of St. Cloud, 2008.

Wolter, Scott Fred, and Richard Nielsen. *The Kensington Rune Stone: Compelling New Evidence*. 1st edition. CreateSpace Independent Publishing Platform, 2006.

The Wine Press by Pre Raphaelite Painter
John Roddam Spencer Stanhope 1864
The inspirational image behind Grapevine Press Ltd.
My concept for the use of this image is that of
the bloodline of Mary Magdalene.

The Templar Quest
to North America - a Photo Journal

Other titles by Gretchen Cornwall

Published by Grapevine Press Ltd. London

The Templar Quest
to North America - a Photo Journal

Sign up for the free newsletter & chapter:
https://gretchencornwall.com/

Follow Ms. Cornwall on Facebook:
https://www.facebook.com/GretchenCornwallAuthor/

Instagram & Twitter

www.ingramcontent.com/pod-product-compliance
Lightning Source LLC
Chambersburg PA
CBHW041957080526
44588CB00021B/2770